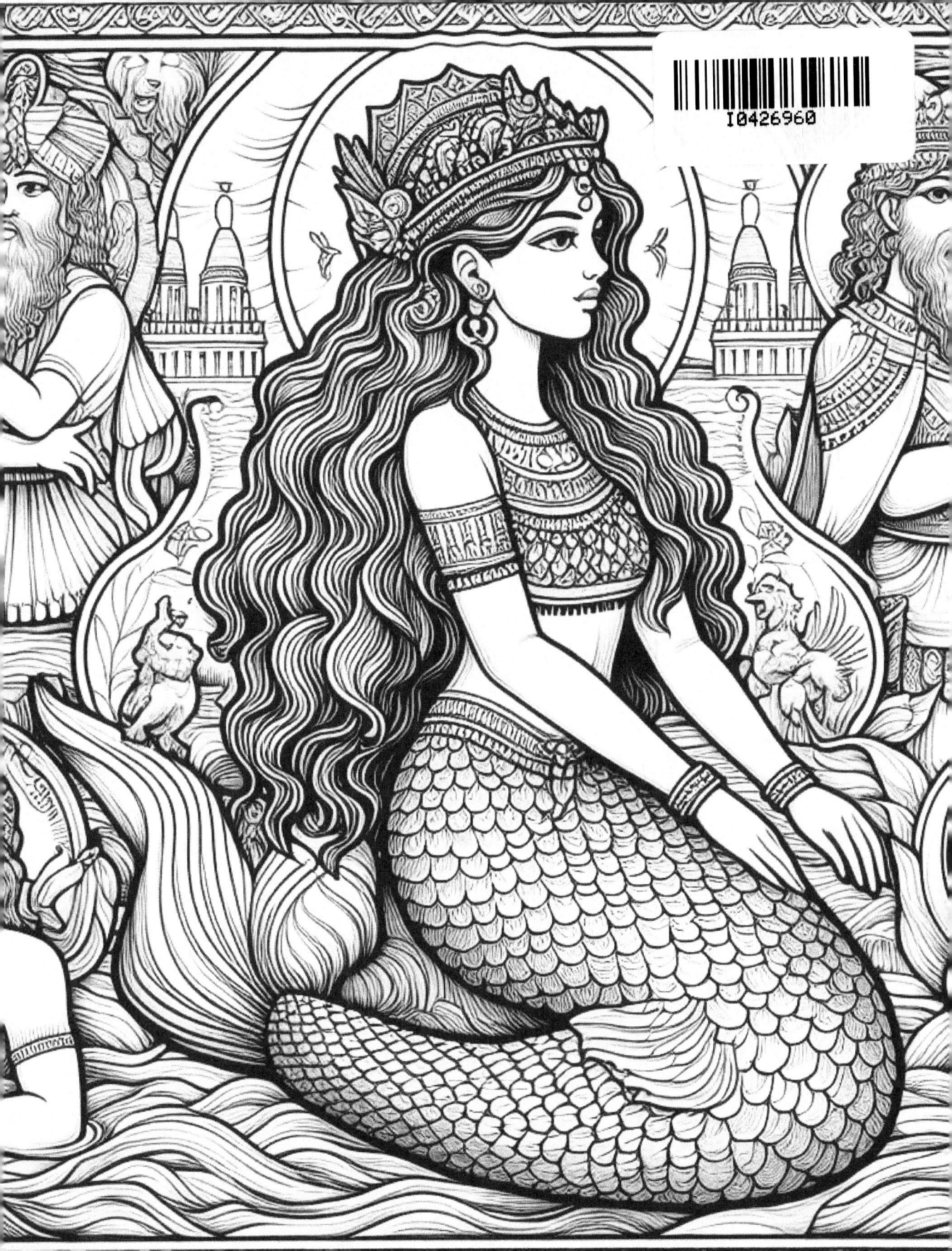

Ancient Assyria

Atargatis

She was a goddess who turned
herself into a mermaid out of remorse
for accidentally killing her lover

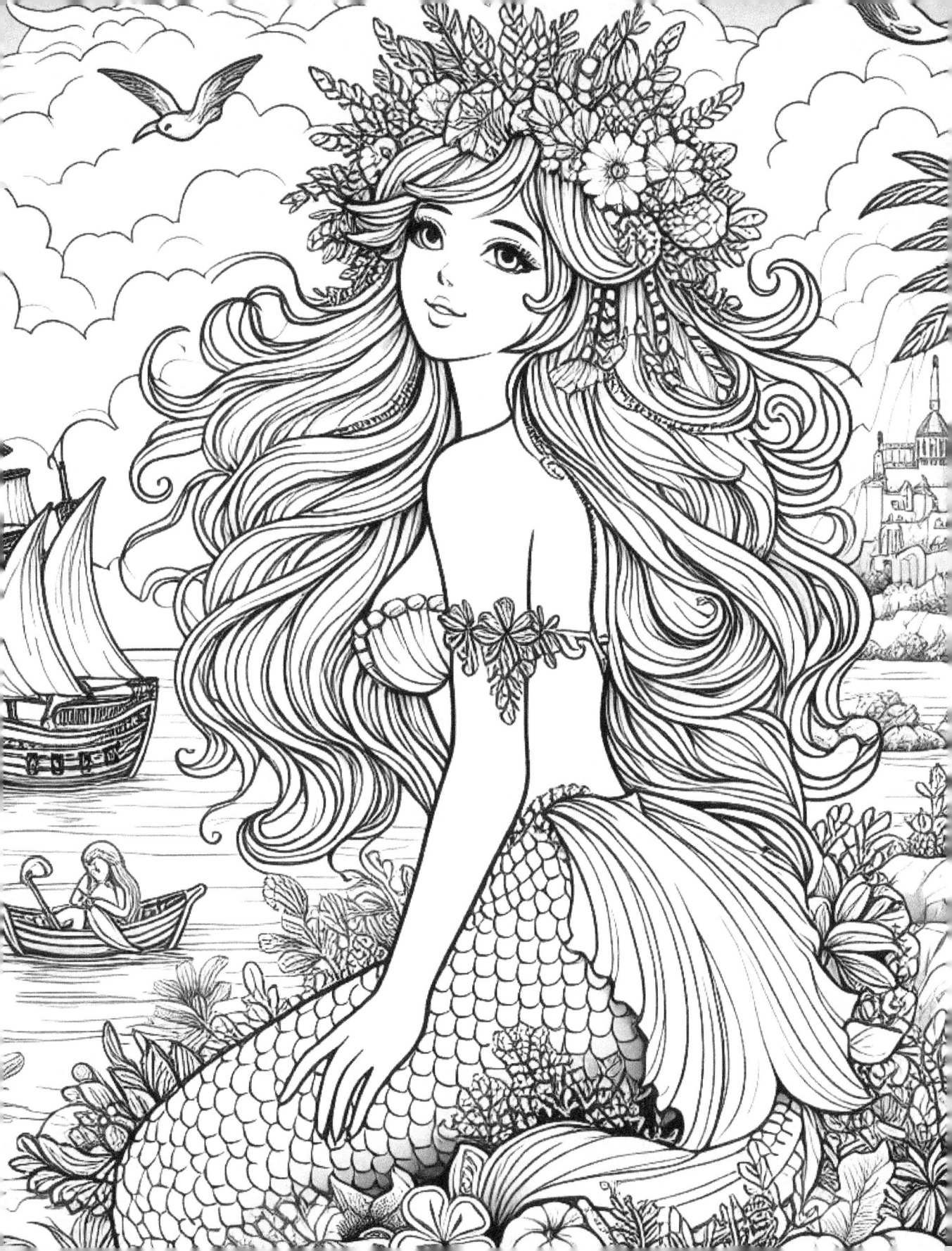

Ancient Greece

Sirens

She was half-human half-bird or half-fish creature who lured sailors to their doom with their enchanting songs

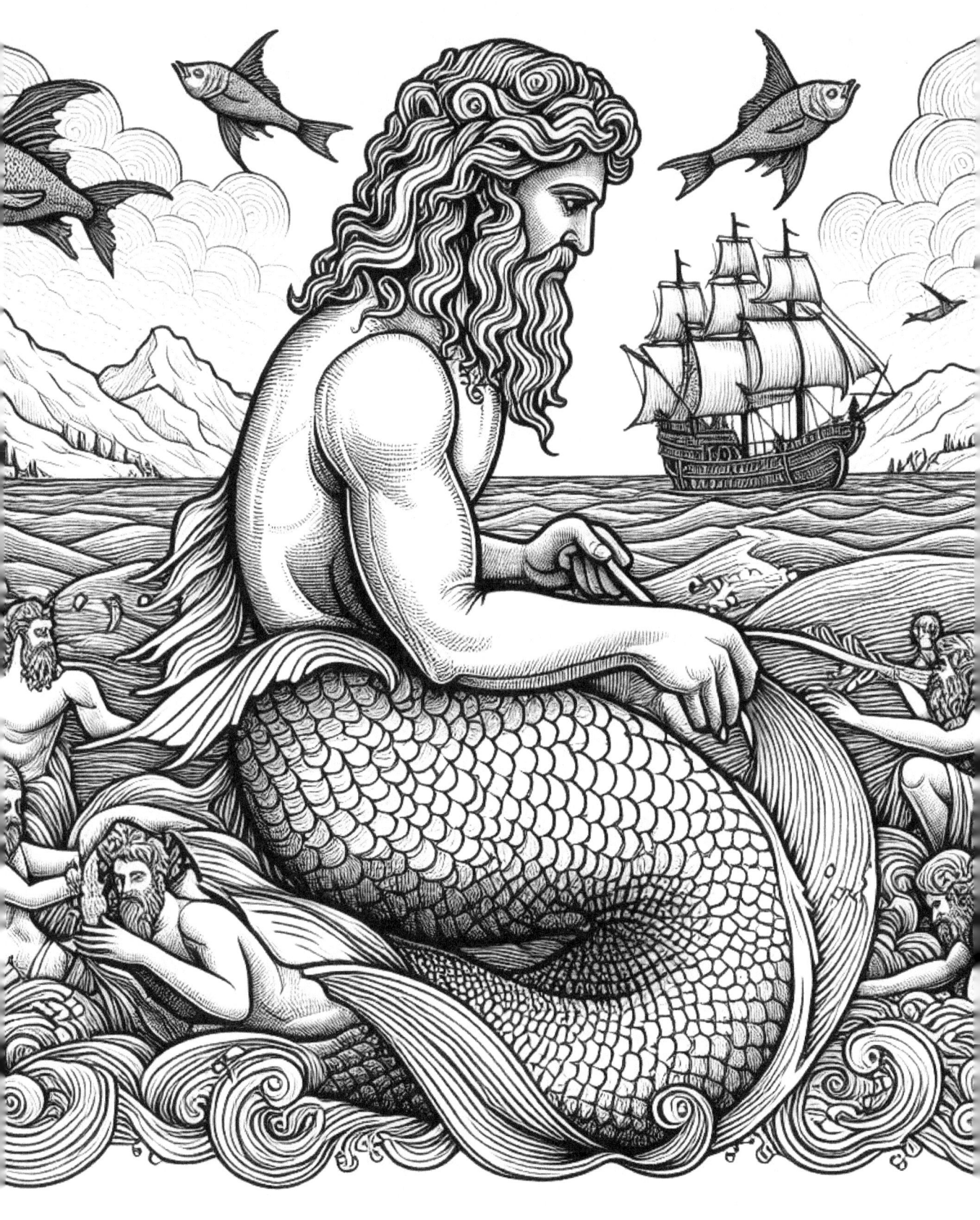

Ancient Greece

Triton

He was the son of the sea god
Poseidon, with human upper body
and fish tail, and served as the
messenger and guardian of the
ocean

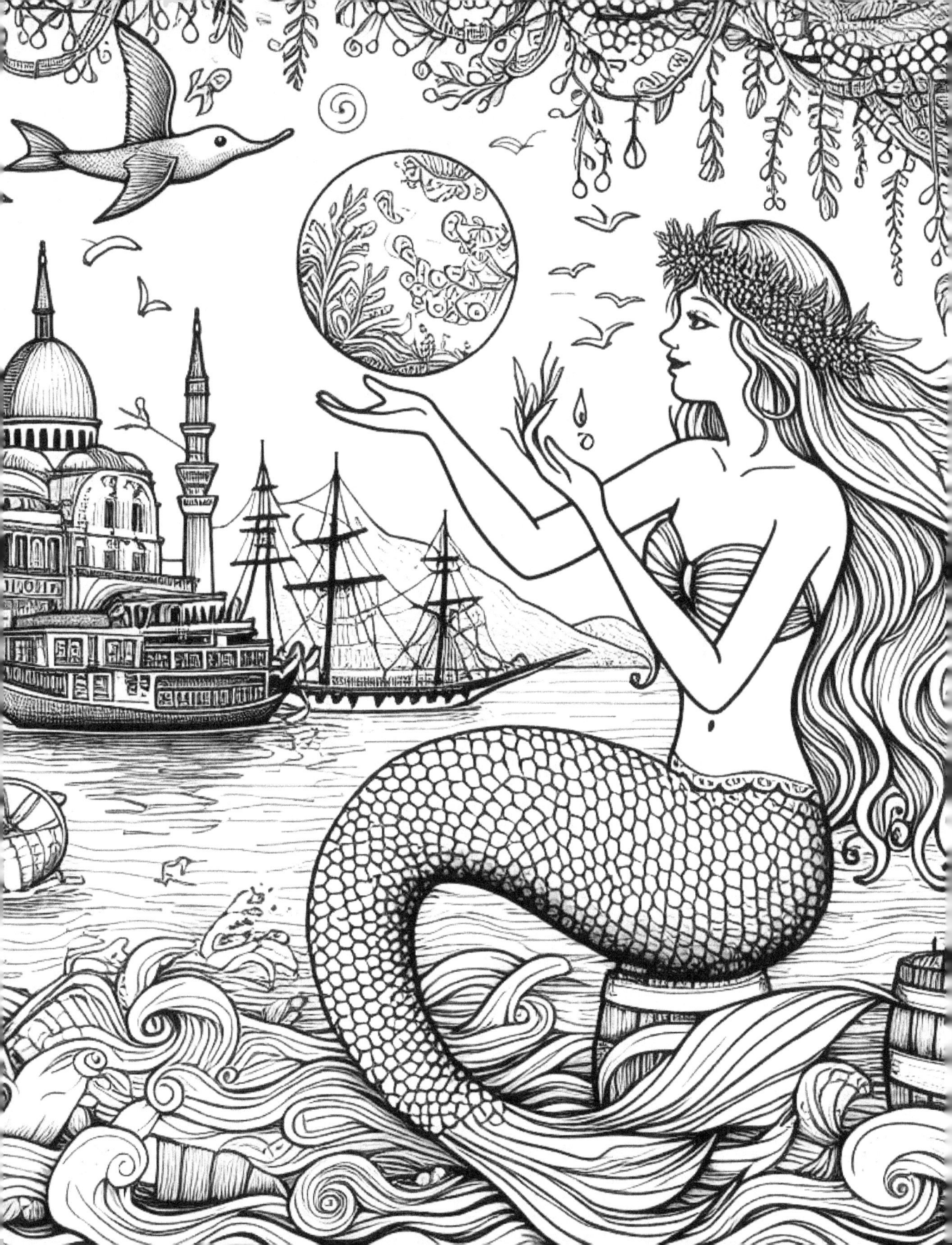

Ancient Greece

Thessalonike

She was the sister of Alexander the Great, who became a mermaid after her death, and asked passing ships: "Is Alexander the king alive?"

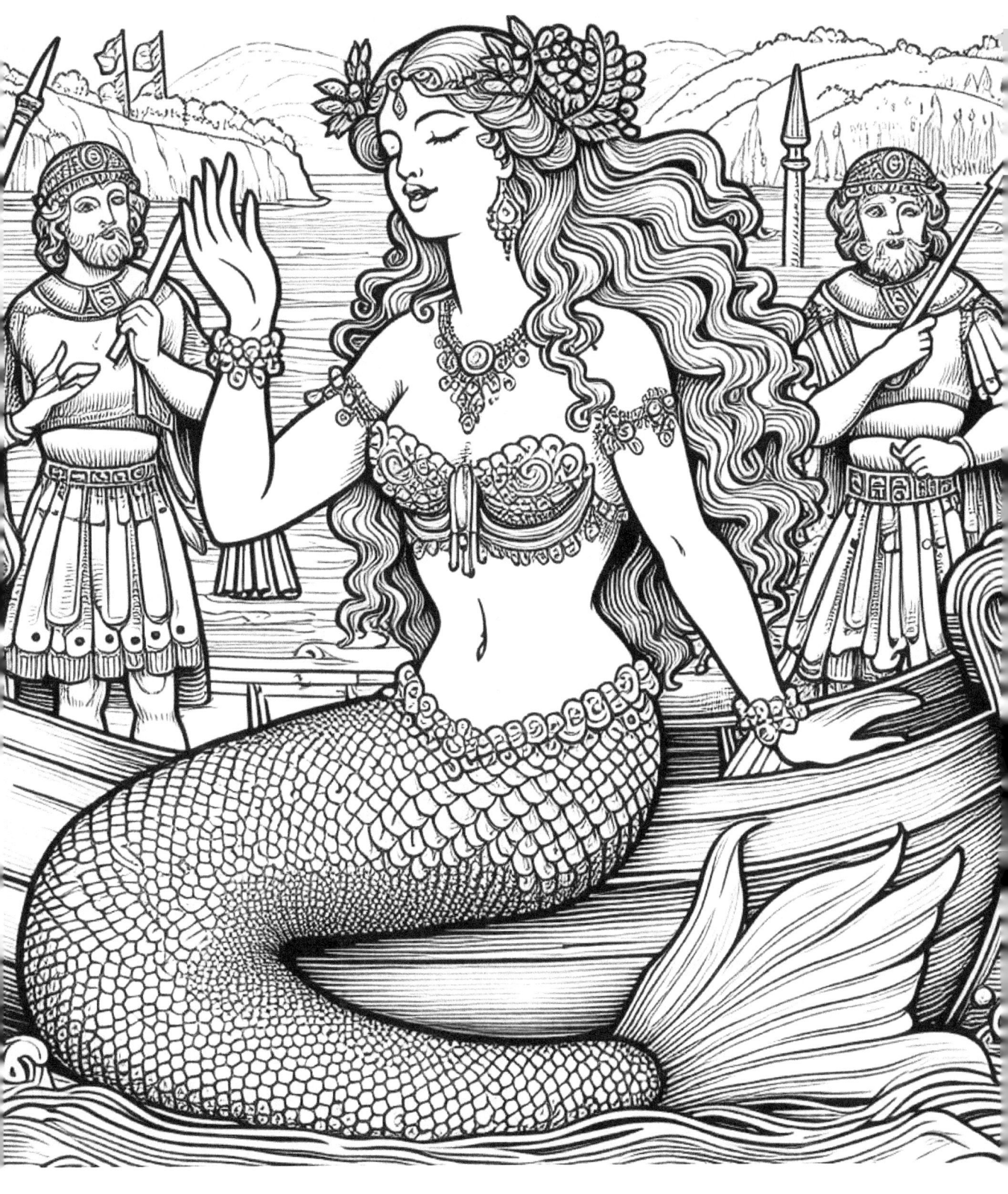

Ancient Rome

Lorelei

She was a mermaid on the Rhine
river, who used her beauty and voice
to bewitch the boatmen, and made
them sink into the river

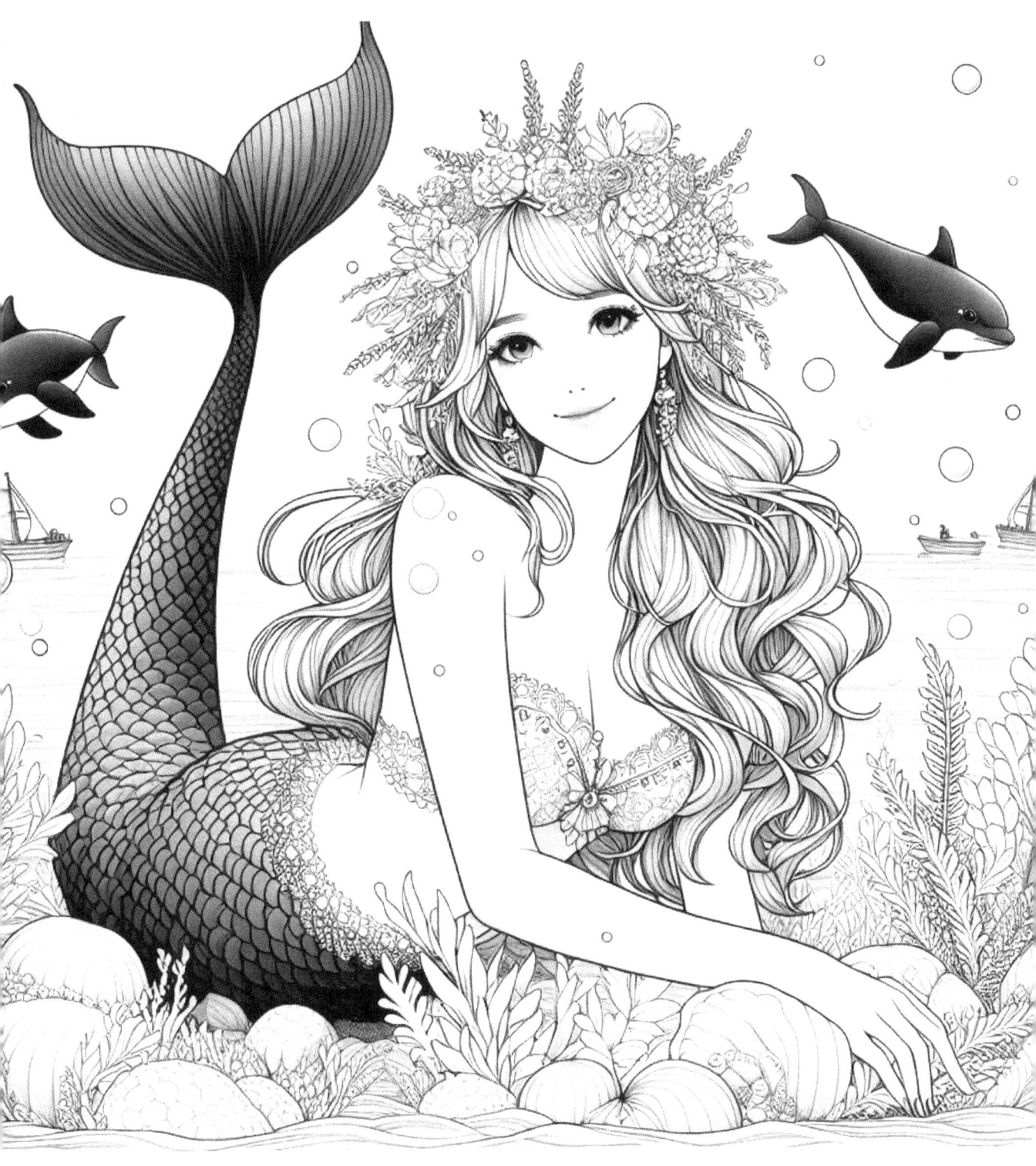

Ireland

Selkie

They were water creatures with human upper bodies and seal tails, who could shed their seal skins and become humans, and marry and have children with humans, but would return to the sea if they lost their seal skins

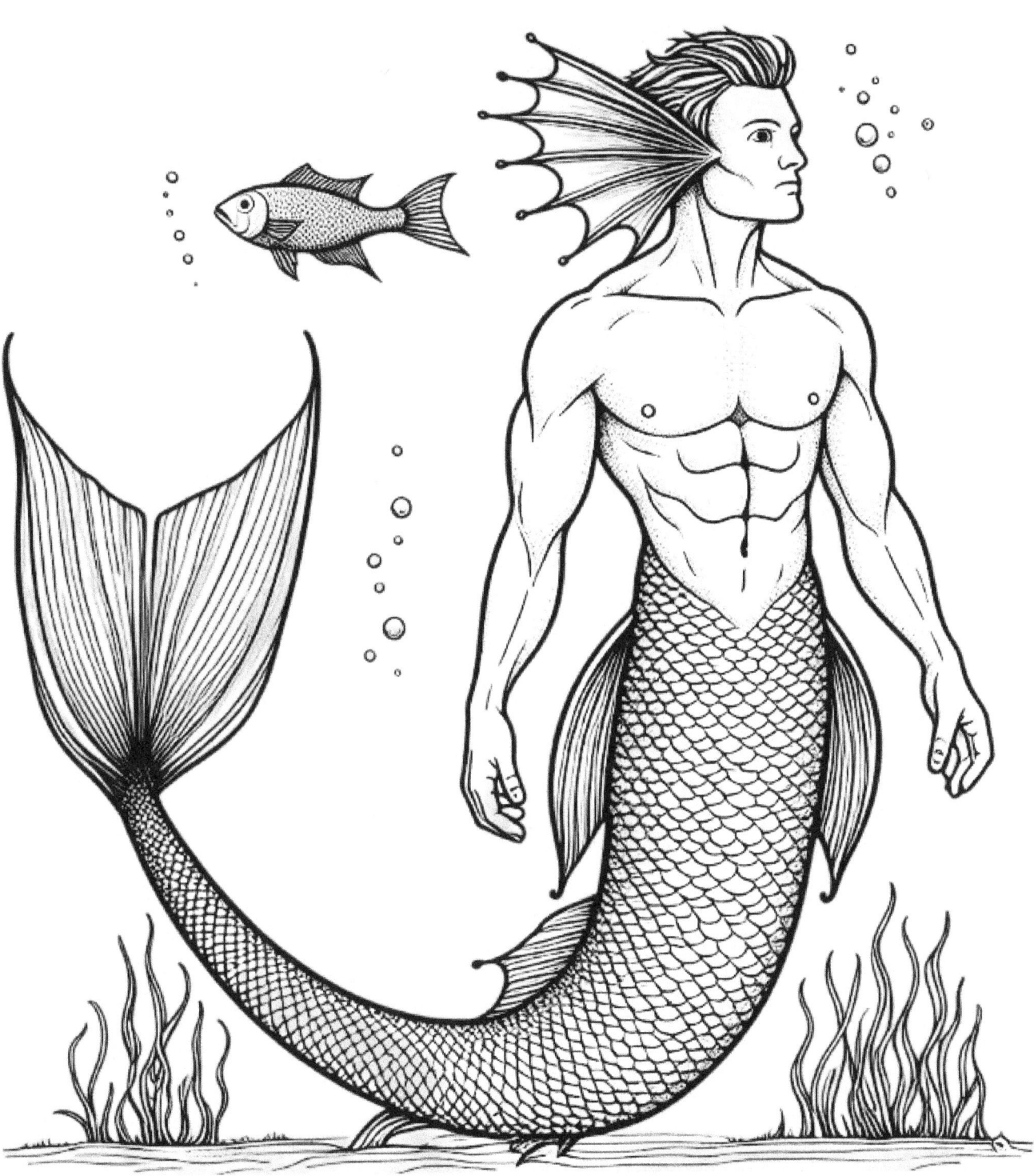

Scotland

Nuckelavee

He was water creature with human
upper body and fish tail, who could
transform into human, and was the
protector of the waters, but also
drowned humans

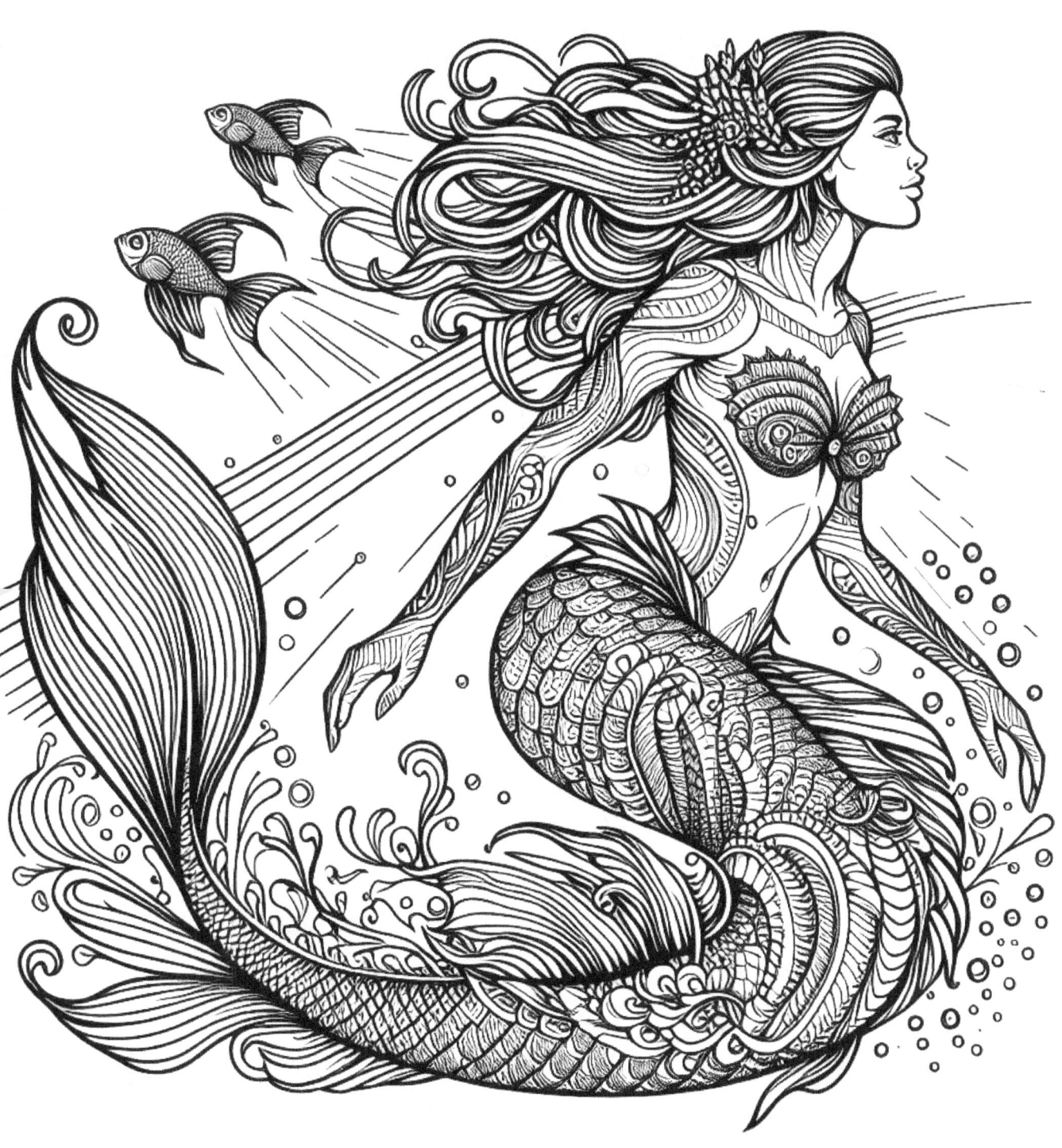

Melanesia

Adaro

She was water creature with human upper bodiy and fish tail, who lived in the sun, and came to earth via rainbows, and was dangerous creature who attacked humans with flying fish

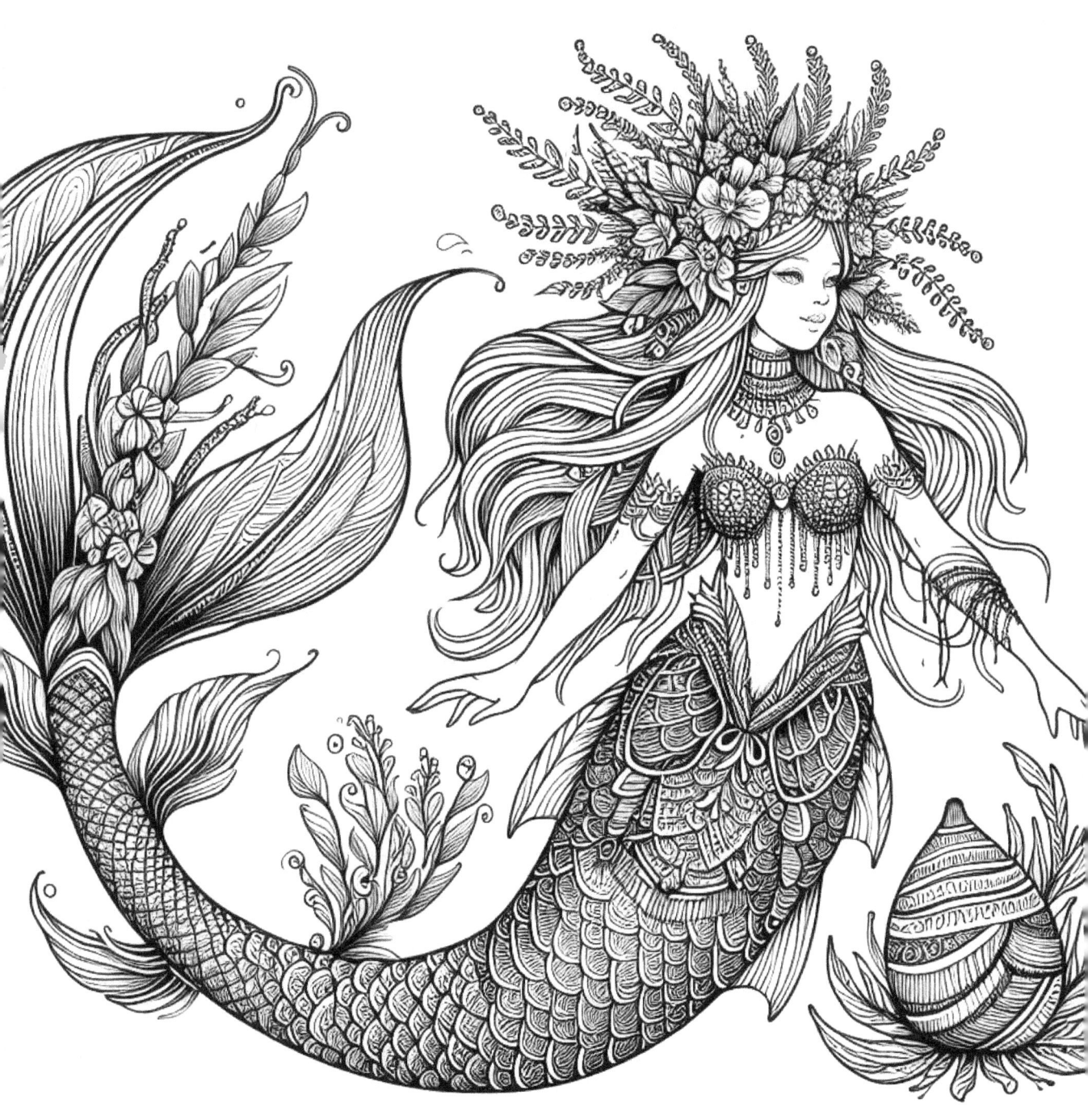

Norway

Havfrue

She was water creature with human
upper body and fish tail, who could
transform into humans, and was the
goddesse of the sea, who could
bless or punish humans

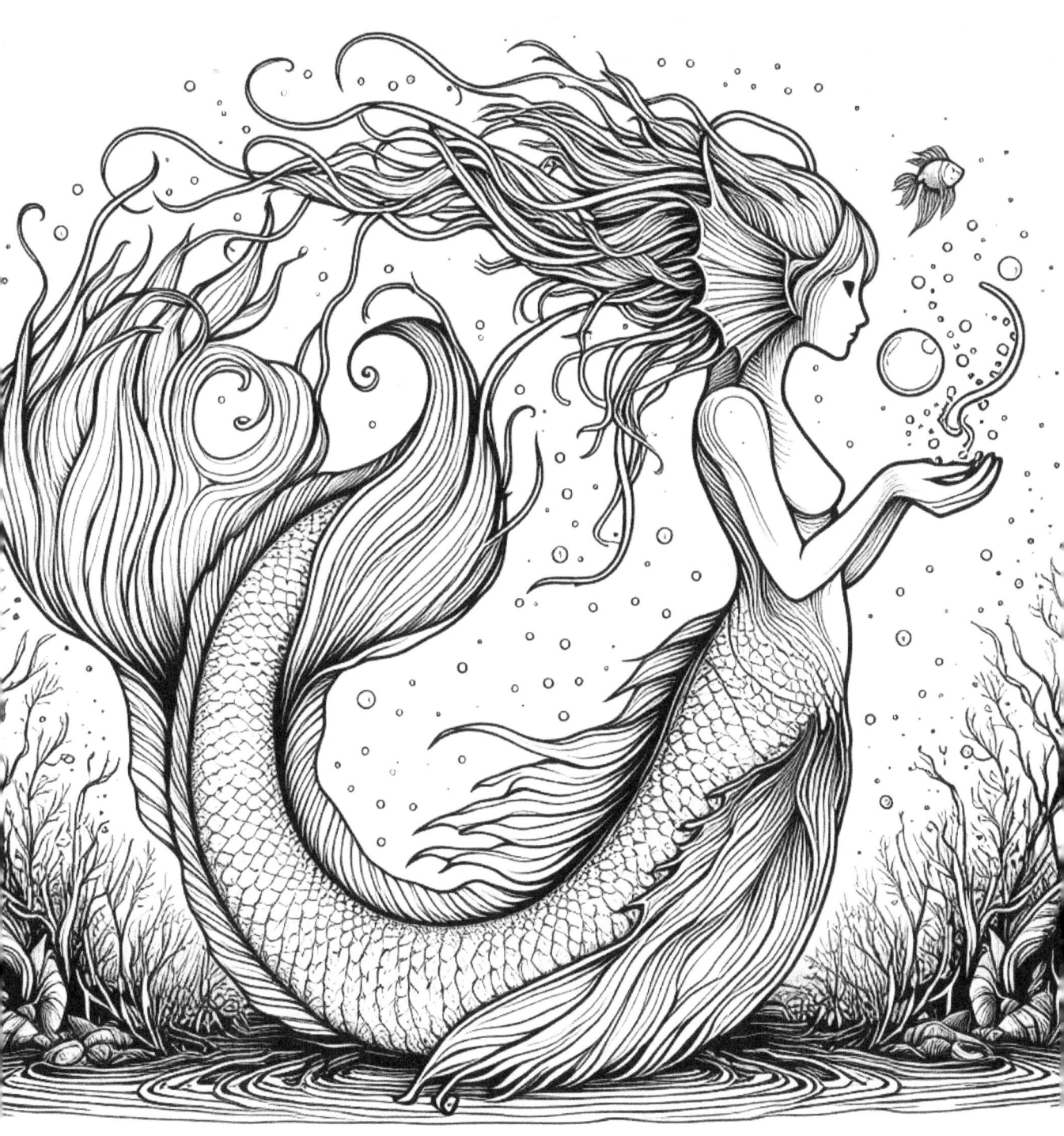

Russia

Rusalka

They were water creatures with
human upper bodies and fish tails,
who could transform into humans,
and were the guardians of the rivers
and lakes, who could heal or kill
humans

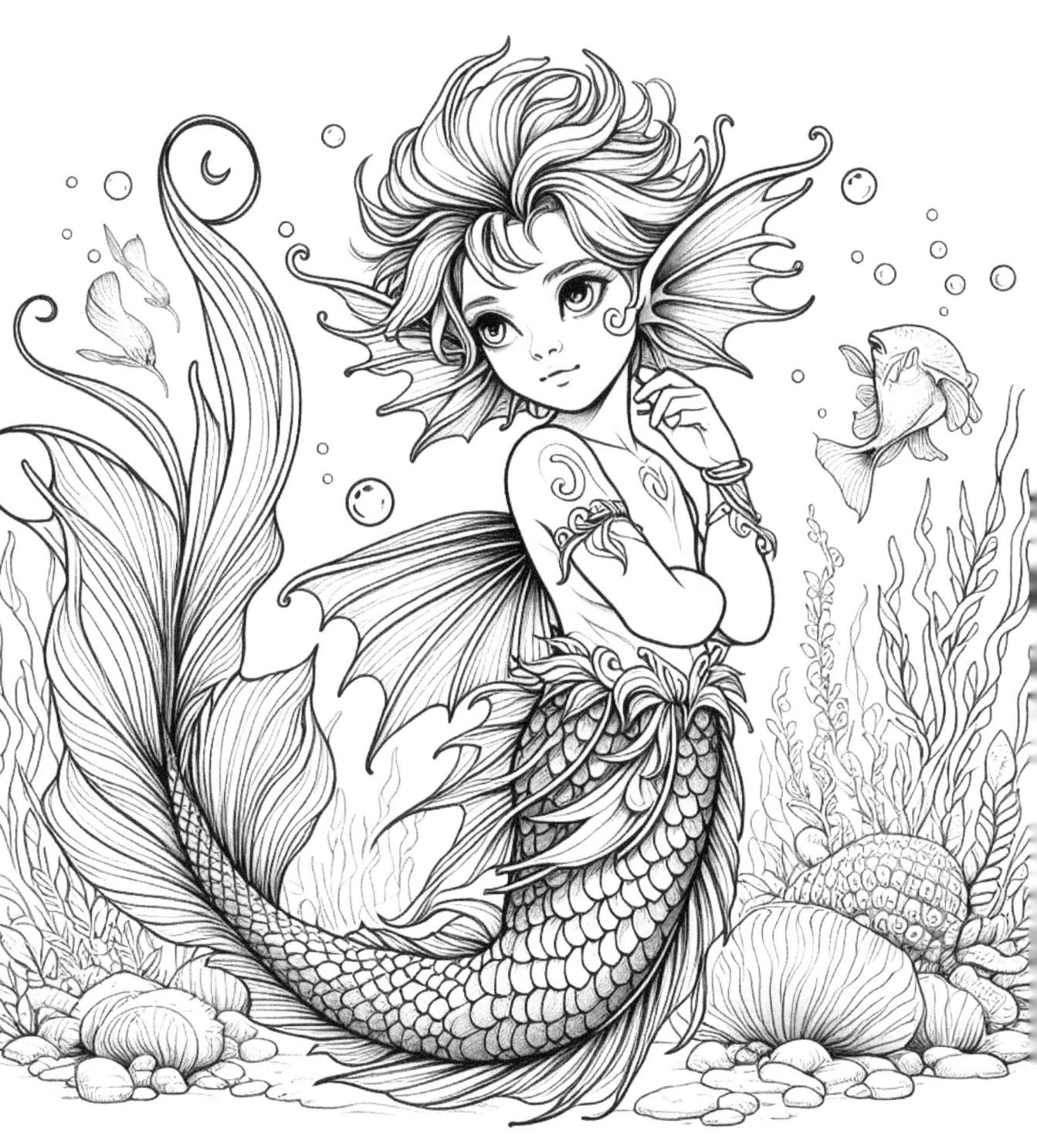

Arabia

Bariya

They were water creatures with
human upper bodies and fish tails,
who could transform into humans,
and were the spirits of the sea, who
could help or deceive humans

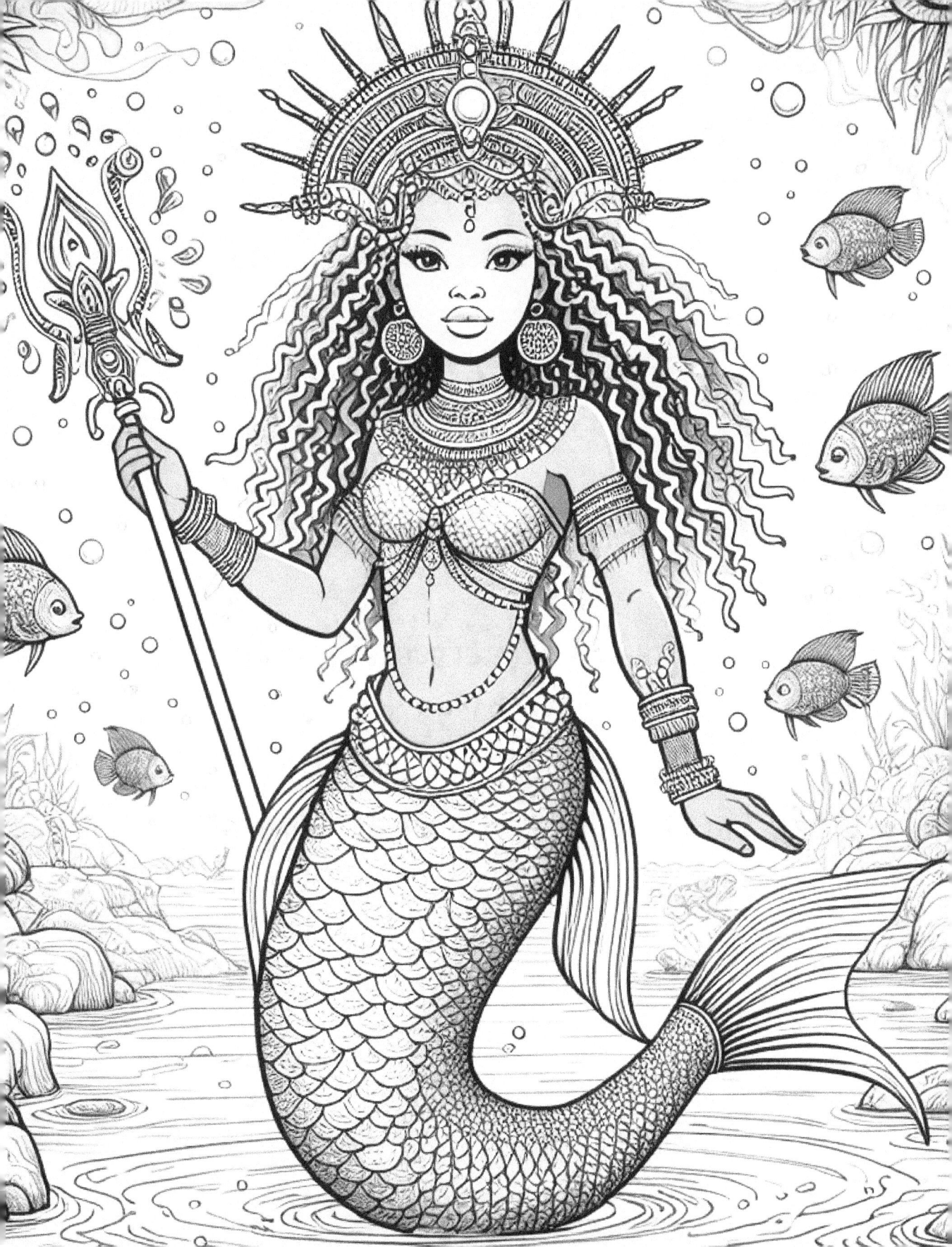

Africa

Mami Wata

She was a water goddess with a
human upper body and a fish tail,
who ruled over the rivers and lakes,
and could bless or punish humans

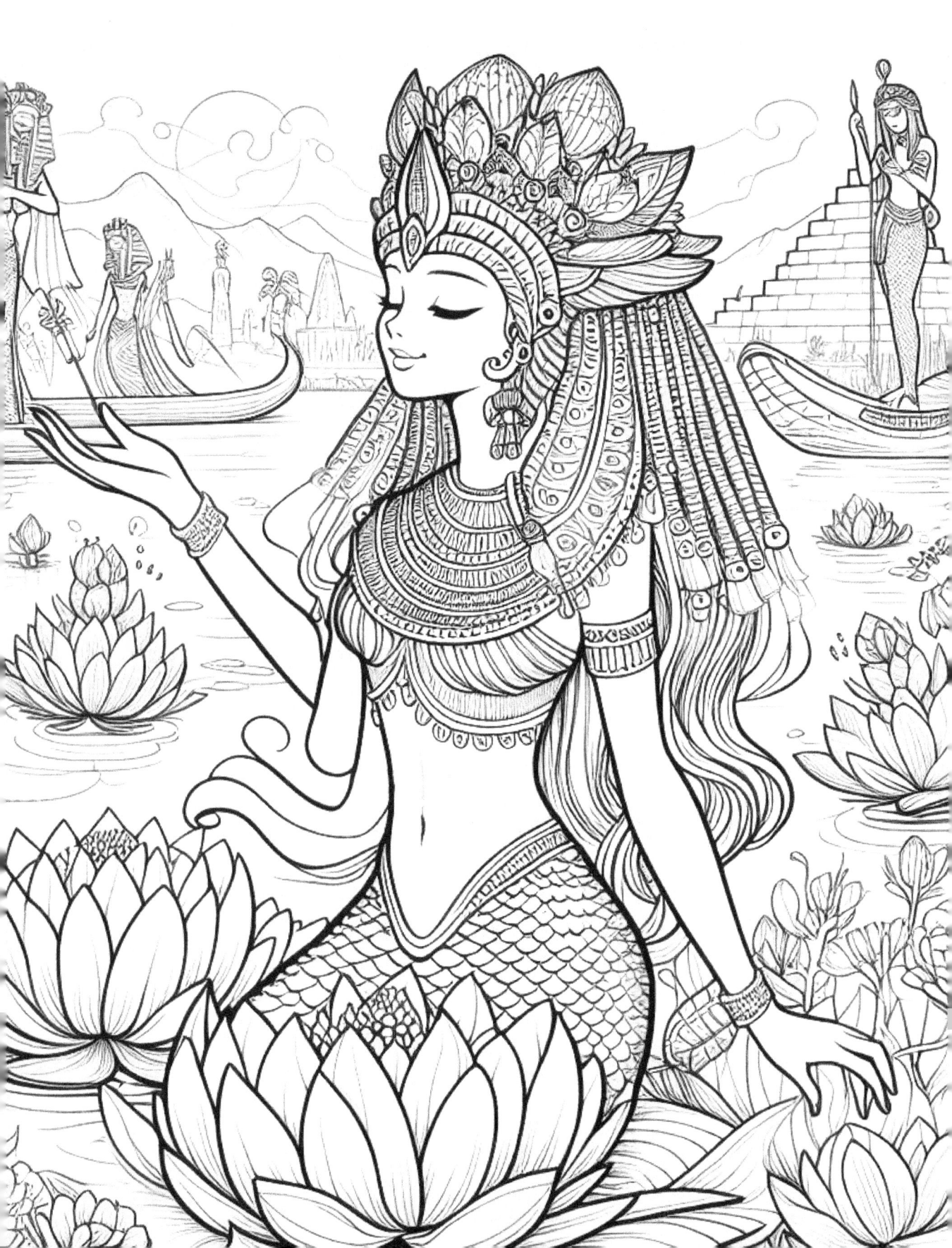

Egypt

Nephthys

She was a goddess who protected the dead and the birth, and was one of the nine pillars of gods in Heliopolis, and helped her sister Isis to preserve and resurrect the body of Osiris

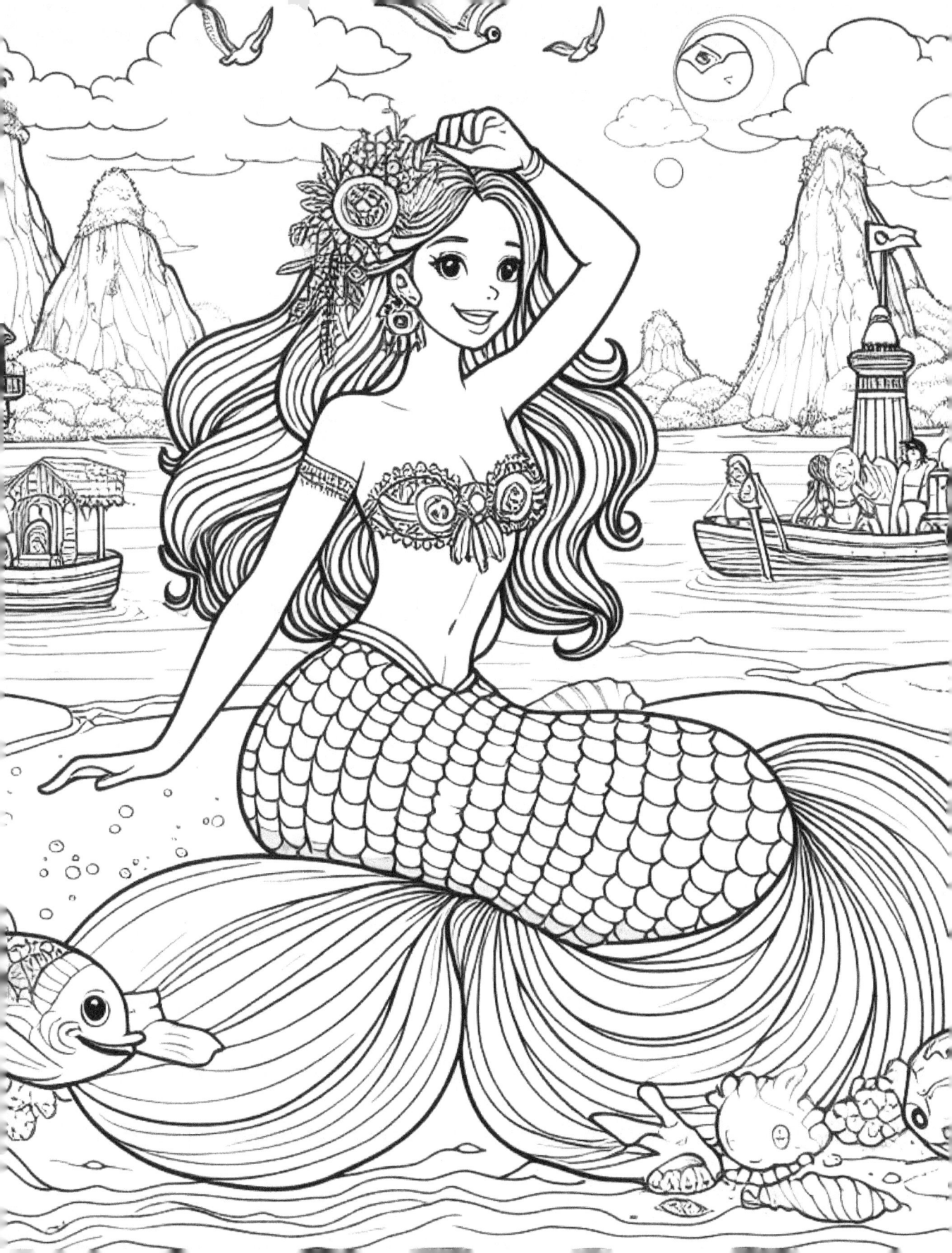

Brazil

Iara

She was a mermaid and the goddess
of the Amazon river, who had green
eyes and black hair, and used her
singing to attract men, and then
took them to the bottom of the river

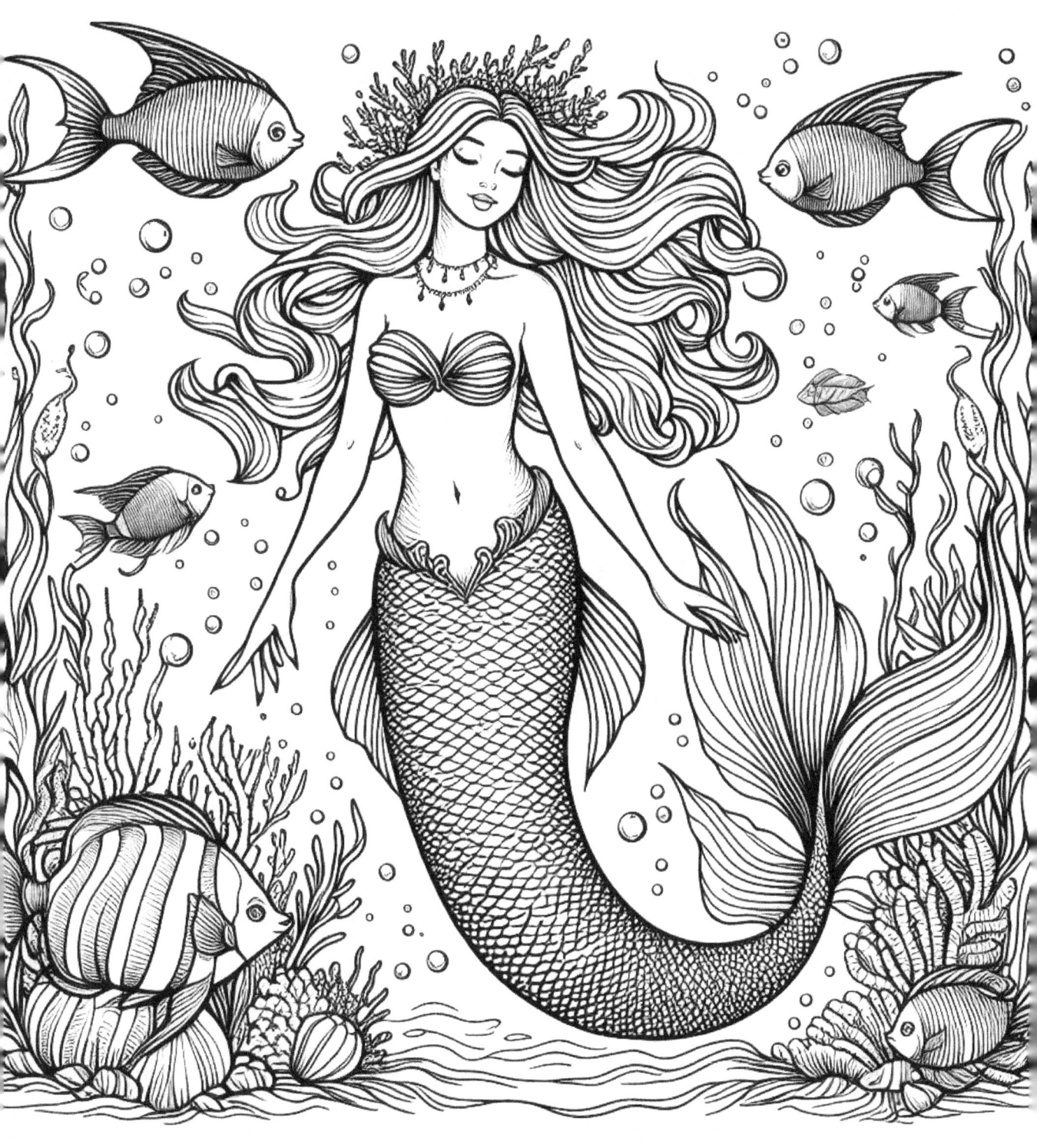

Colombia

Mohana

They were water creatures with
human upper bodies and fish tails,
who could transform into humans,
and were the goddesses of the rivers
and lakes, who could seduce or
drown humans

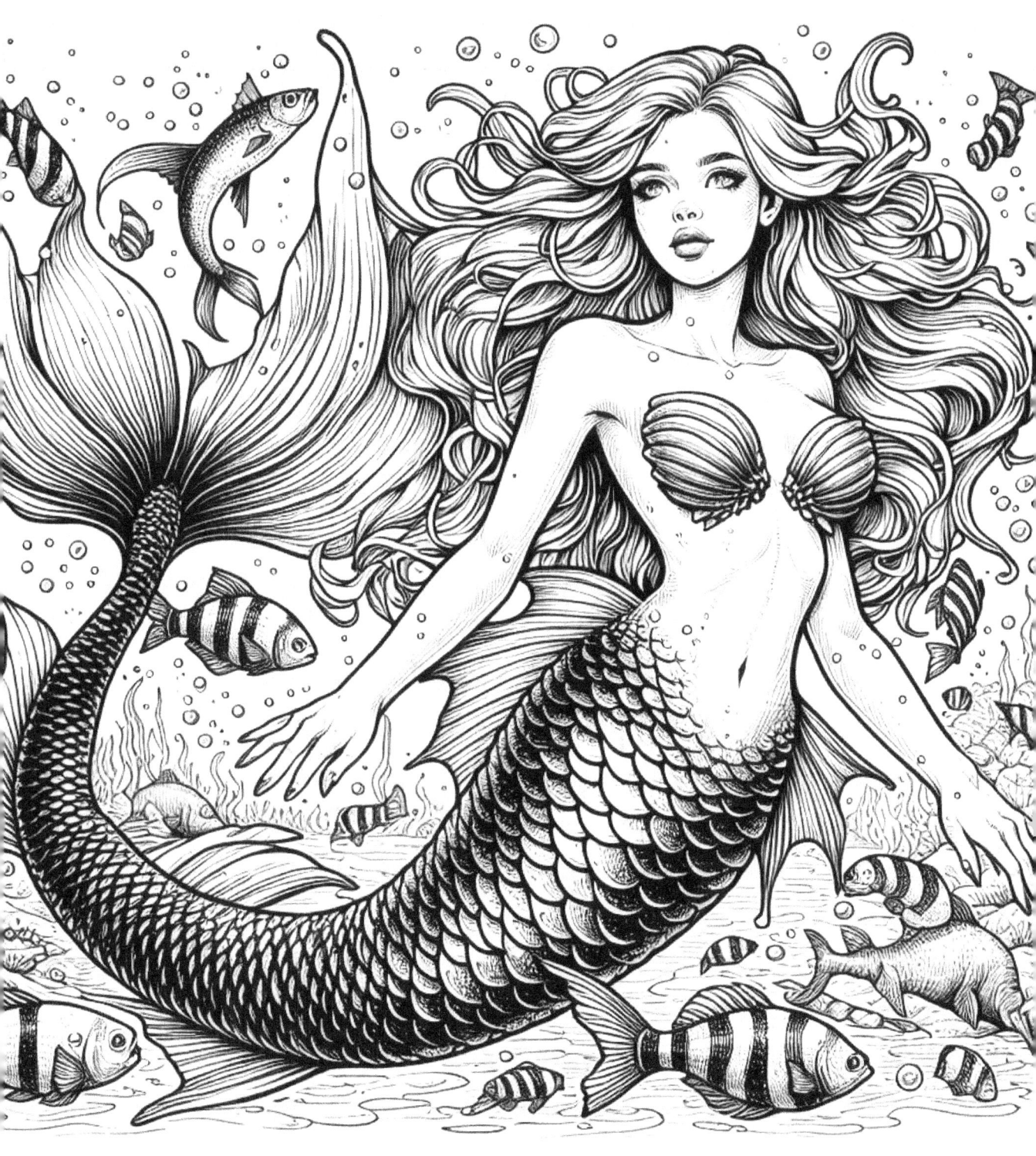

Mermaid

They were water creatures with
human upper bodies and fish tails,
who could transform into humans,
and were the spirits of the sea, who
could love or kill humans

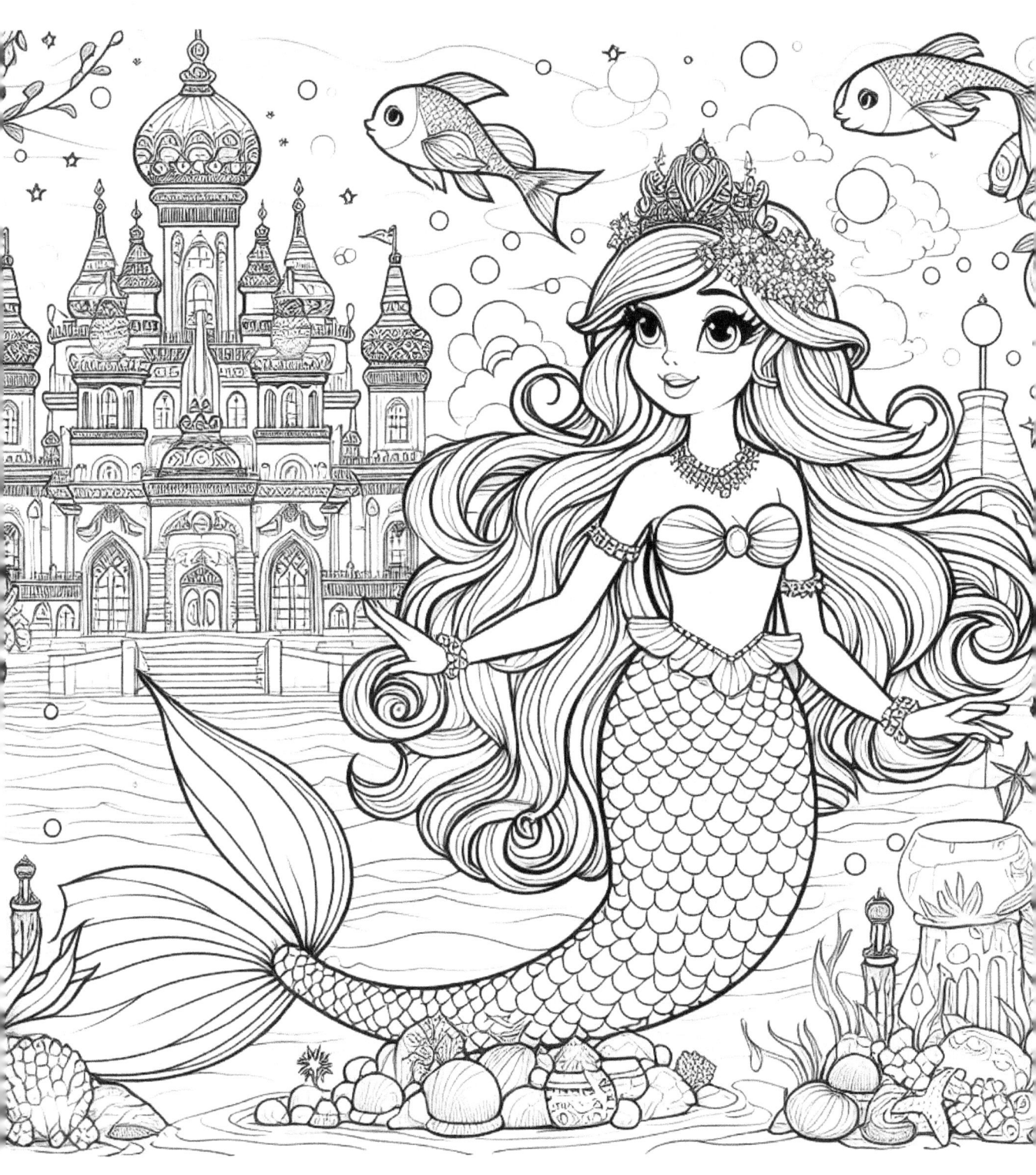

Denmark

The Little Mermaid

She was a mermaid who traded her
voice for a human form, and fell in
love with a human prince, but the
prince did not love her back, and she
turned into foam

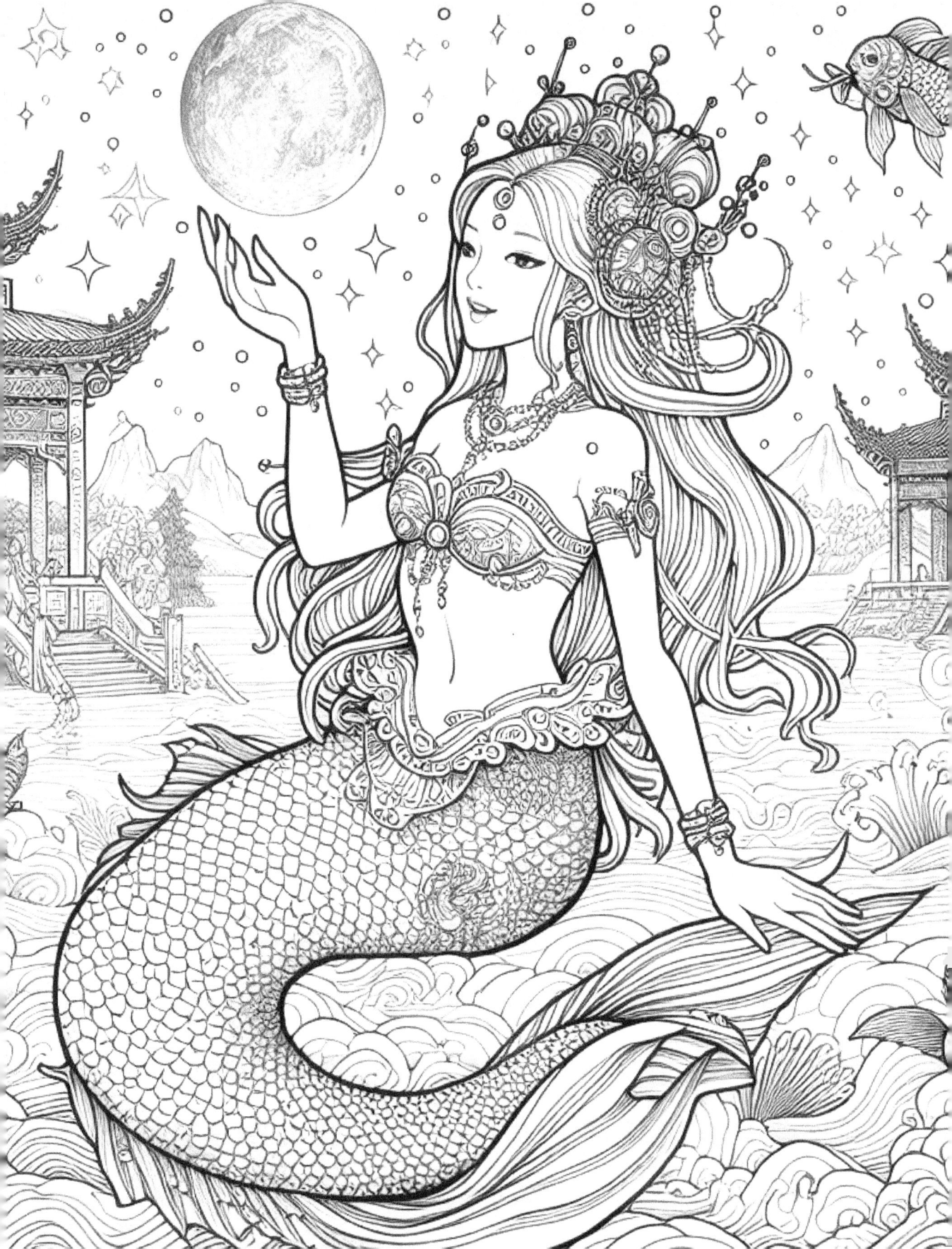

China

Beauty under the moon

She was a water spirit who
transformed into a human on every
full moon night, and fell in love with
humans

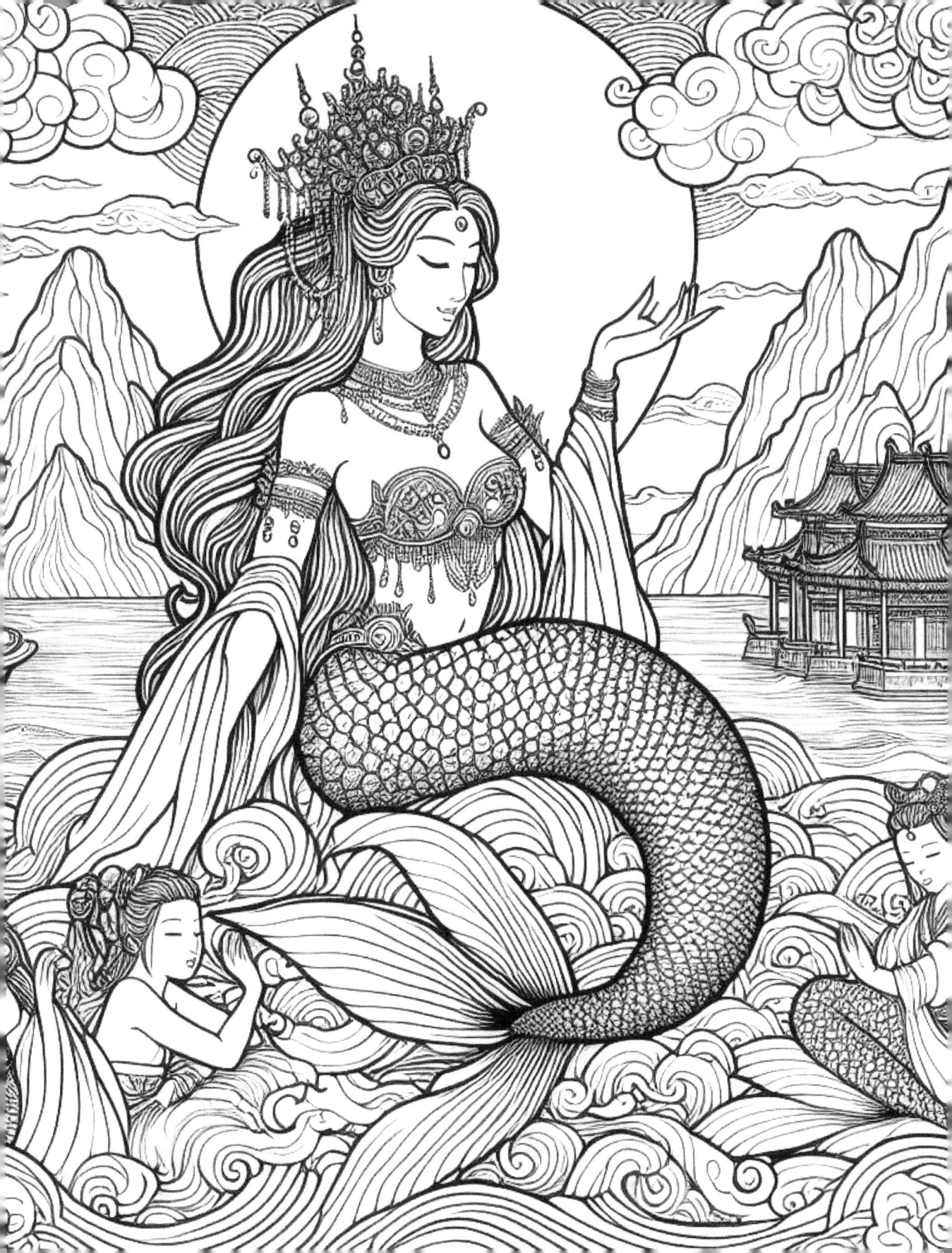

China 《The Classic of Mountains and Seas》

Shark people

They are a kind of aquatic creature, with a human body and a fish tail, living in the sea, able to transform into a human form, marry and have children with humans, but if they lose their fish tail, they will die

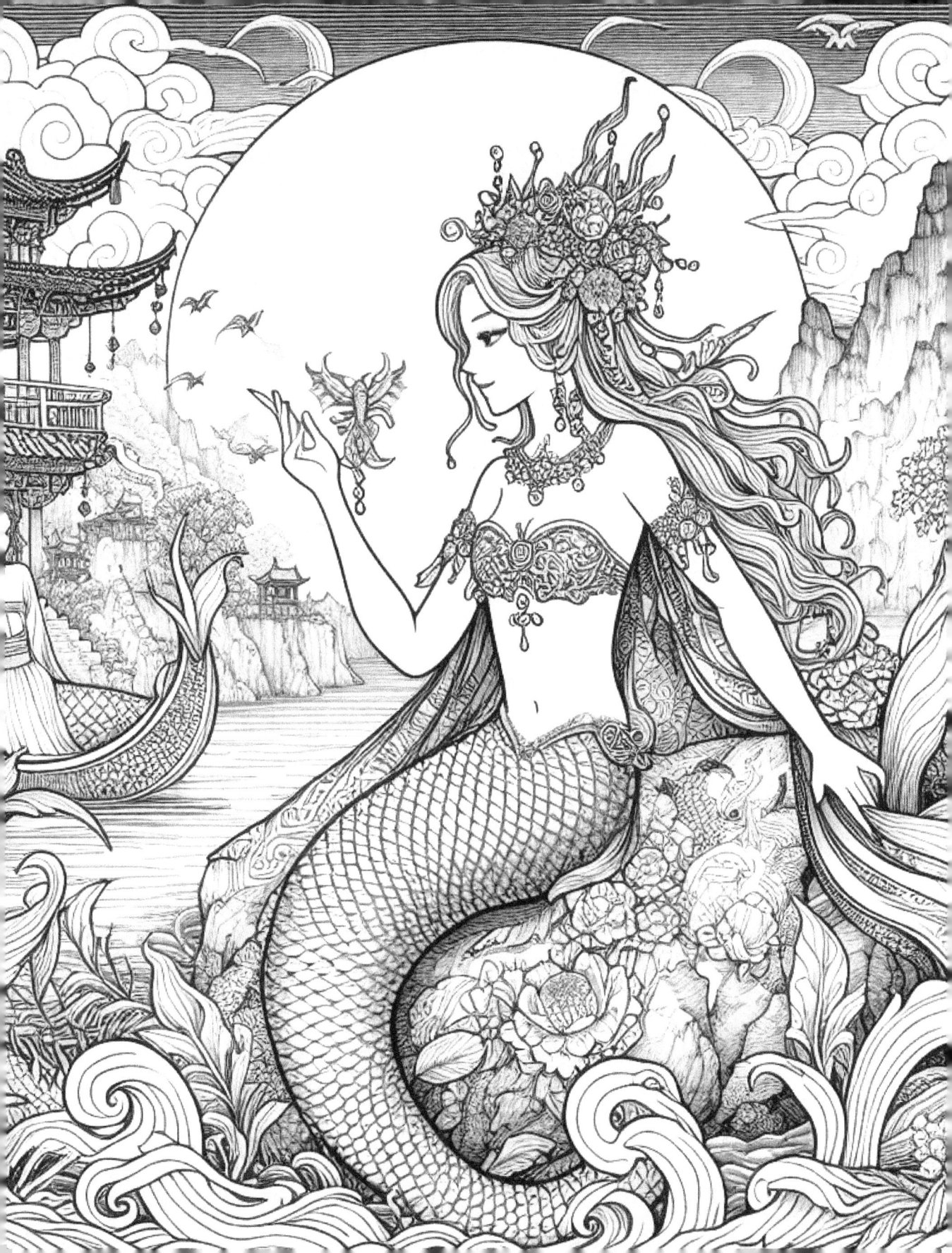

China 《The Classic of Mountains and Seas》

Fish Woman

She is a kind of aquatic creature, with a human body and a fish tail, living in the sea, able to transform into a human form, marry and have children with humans, but if her true identity is discovered, she will be killed

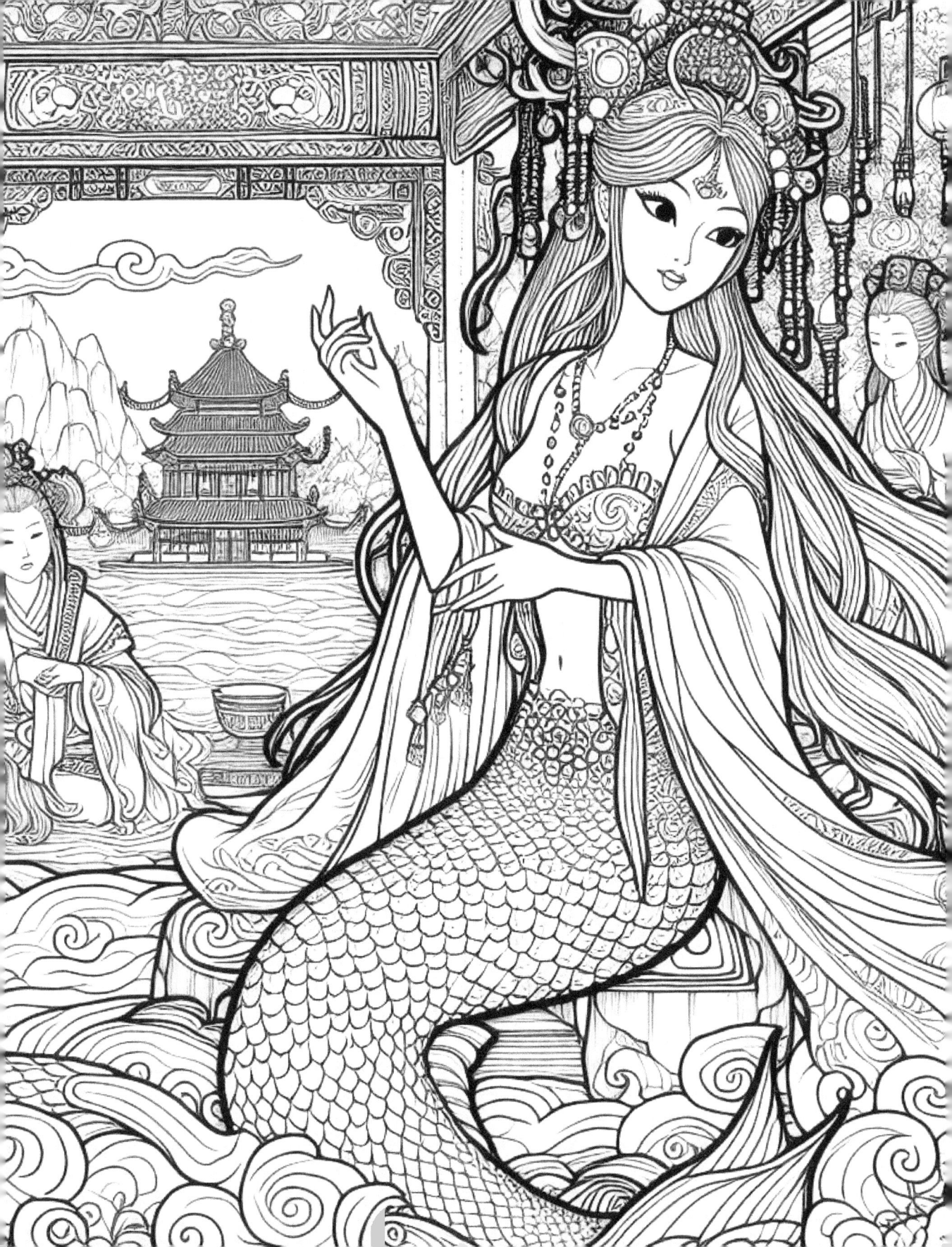

China 《Strange Tales from a Chinese Studio》

Flower girl

She is a mermaid, who fell in love
with a human scholar, and
exchanged her fish tail for a human
form, and loved the scholar, but the
scholar's mother discovered her
secret, and wanted to kill her

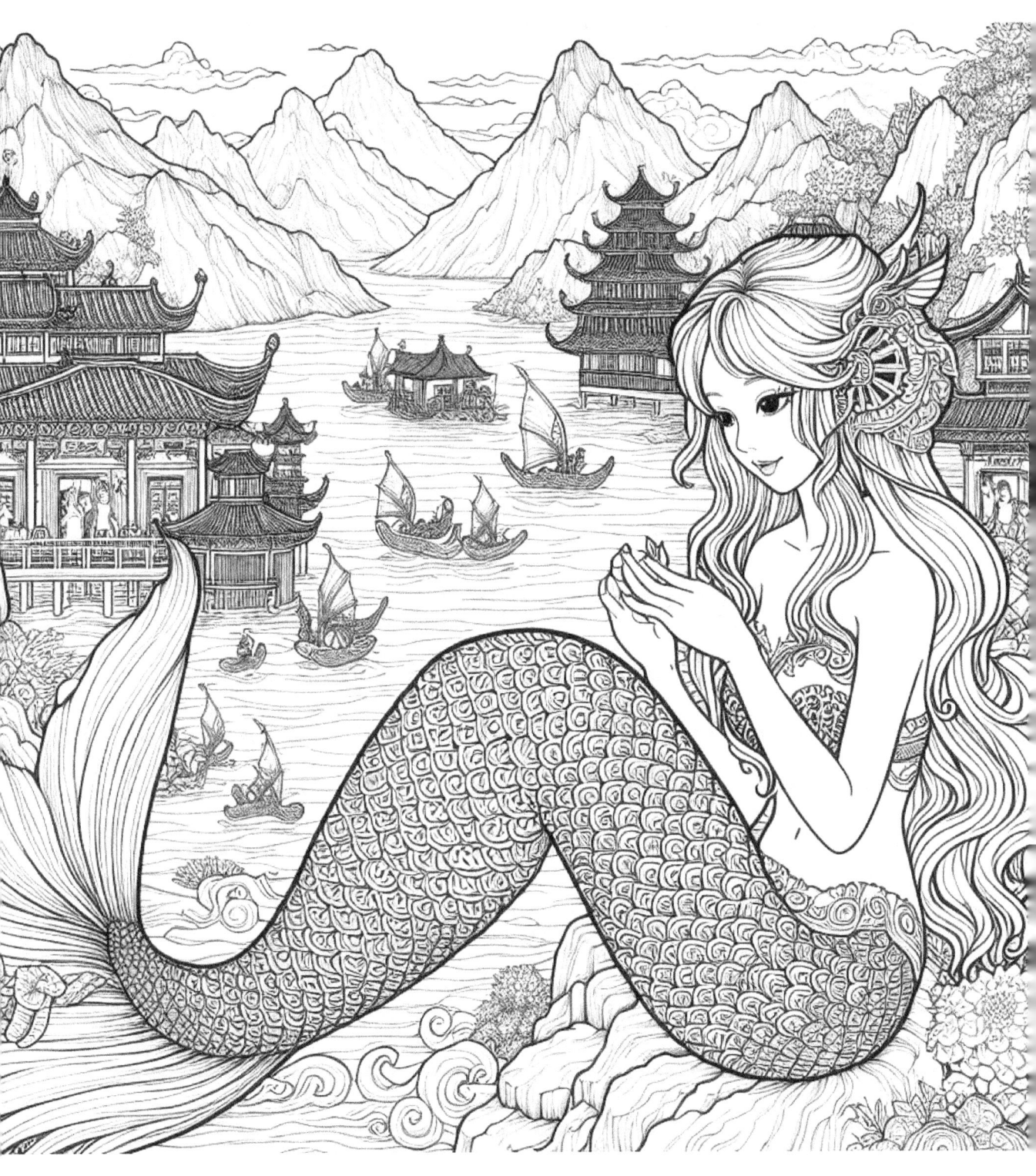

China 《Extensive Records of the Taiping Era》

sea fish man

They are a kind of aquatic creature, with a human body and a fish tail, living in the East Sea, with graceful appearance, long hair over the waist, kept by the widowed and lonely people along the coast,

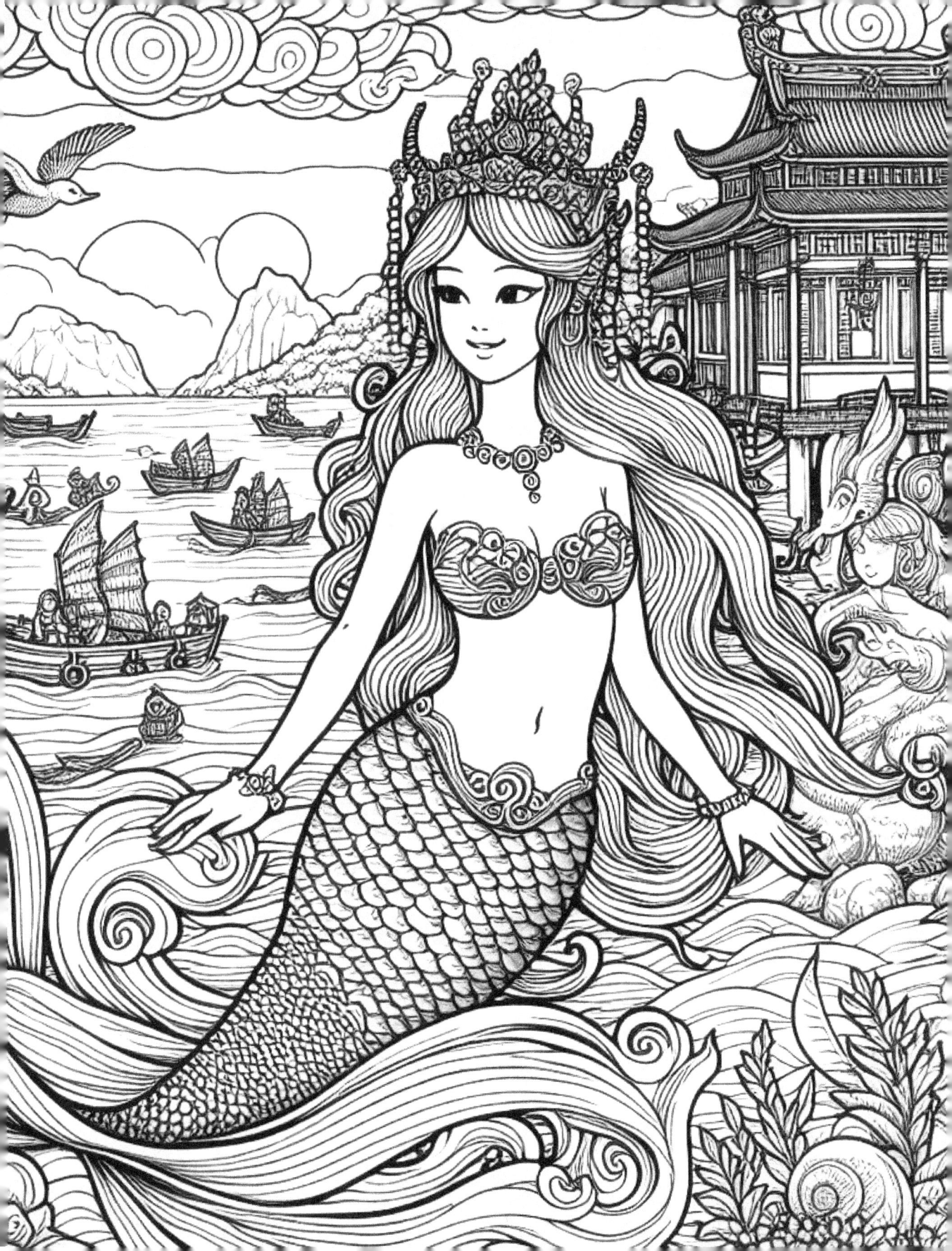

China 《Extensive Records of the Taiping Era》

Lu Ting

They are a kind of aquatic creature, with a human body and a fish tail, living in rivers and lakes, with a very short tail, very timid, harmless, playing with sailors, and not harming them until the end of the voyage

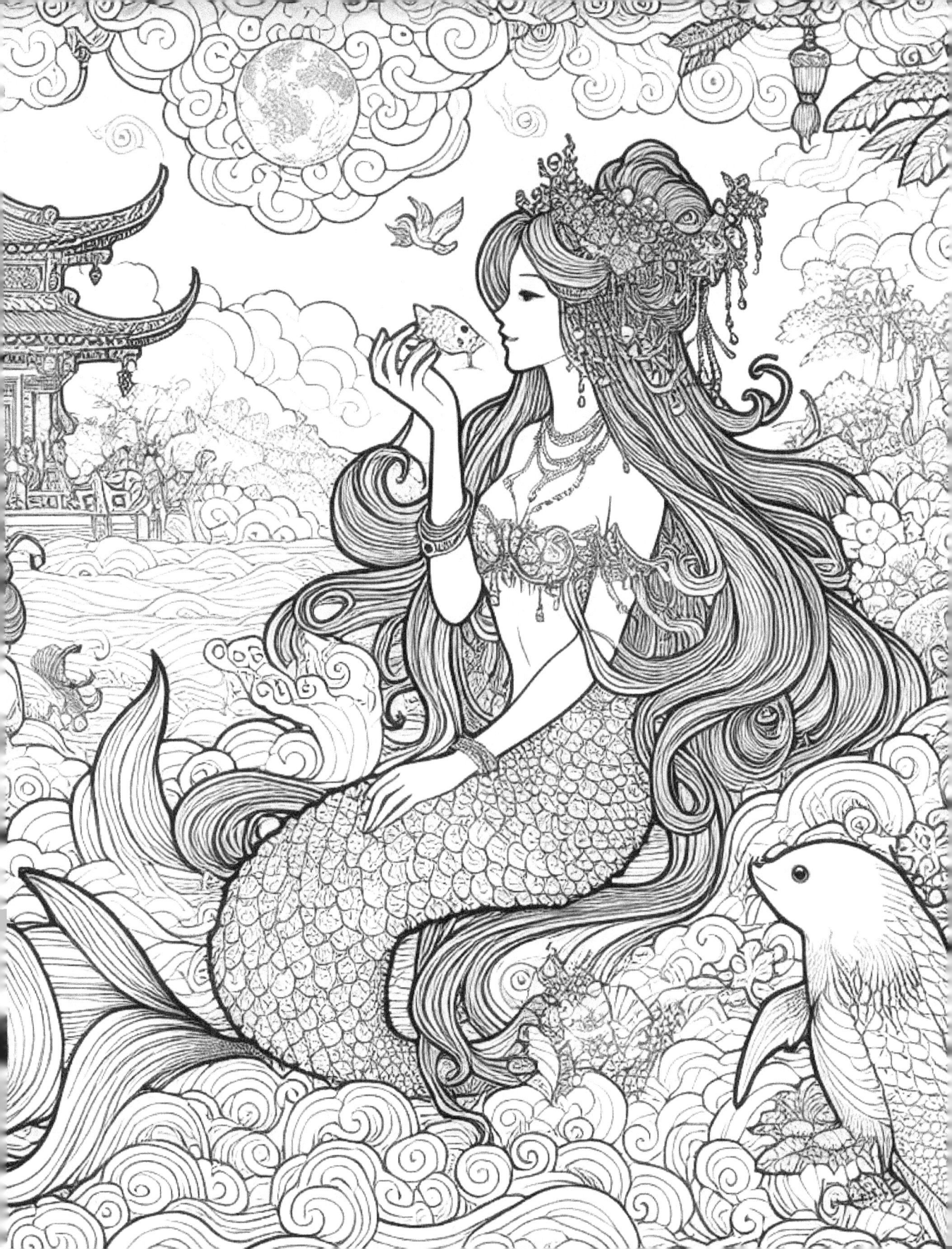

China 《Extensive Records of the Taiping Era》

Jiang Huang

She is a kind of aquatic creature, with a human body and a fish tail, living in the Yangtze River, with a beautiful and seductive appearance, and also knows magic, was captured and tortured by a rogue ruffian, and the ruffians were infected with a bad disease, which was the punishment of the mermaid for them

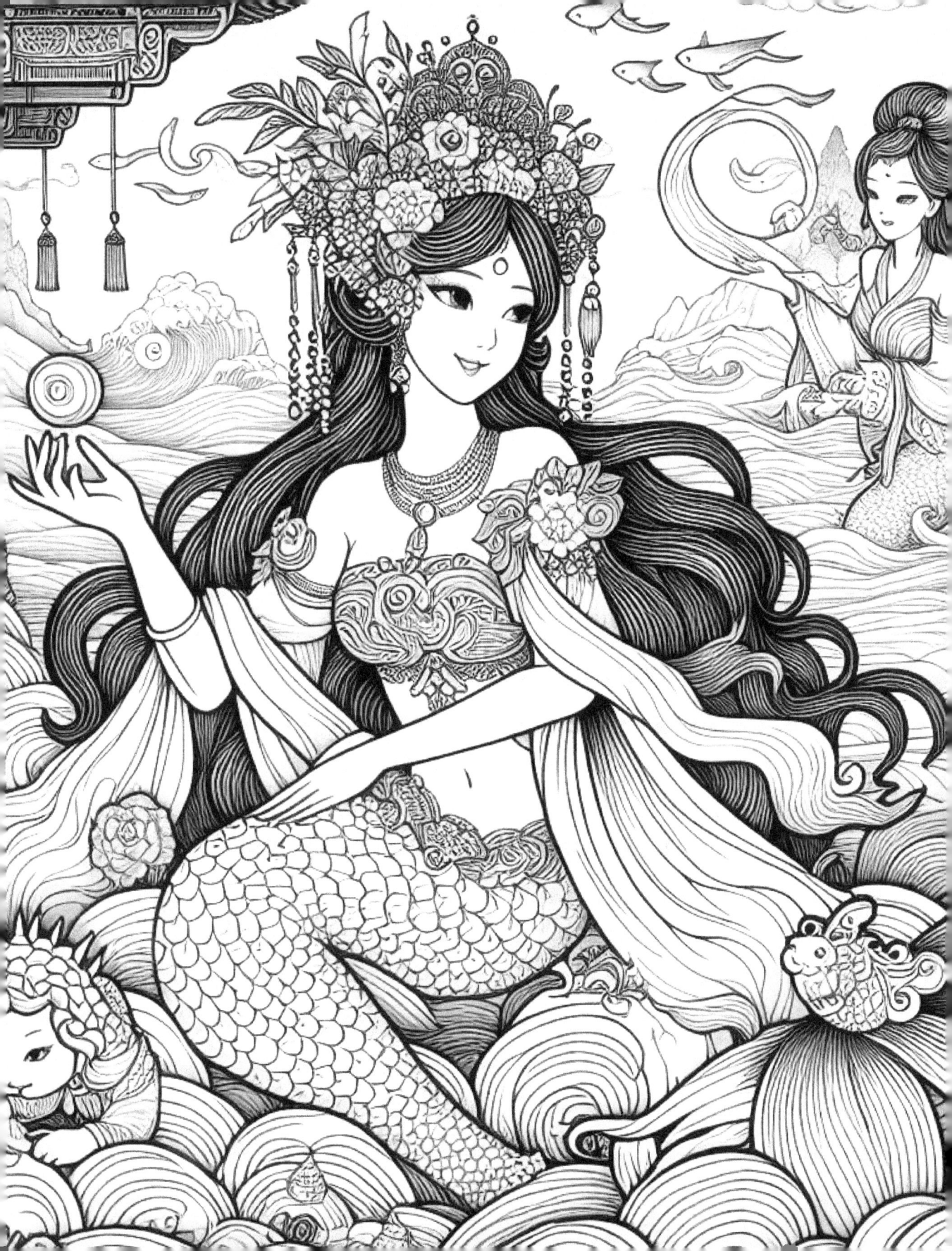

China 《News of the Conversation》

Jiang Huang

She is a kind of aquatic creature,
with a human body and a fish tail,
living in the sea, captured by a
fishing boat, a scholar gave her wine
and soup to drink, she got drunk and
cried, and finally was released

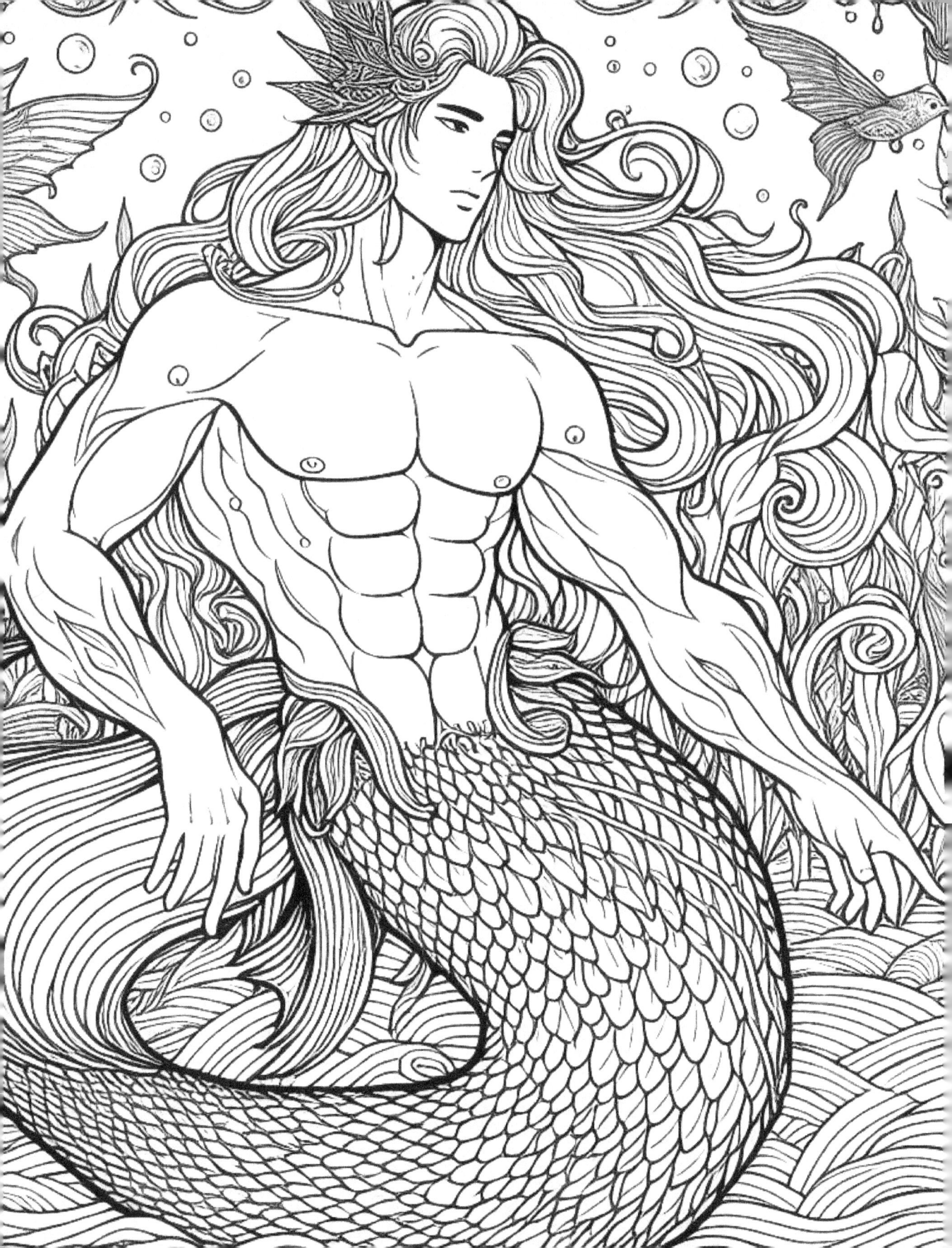

China 《Narrative of Differences》

Quanxian

There are shark people in the South China Sea, as a fish-shaped, haunted the sea, can spin and weave, cry when crying, its tears are beads, the beads are as big as chicken eggs, its color is blue and white, its light is human, and its price is invaluable

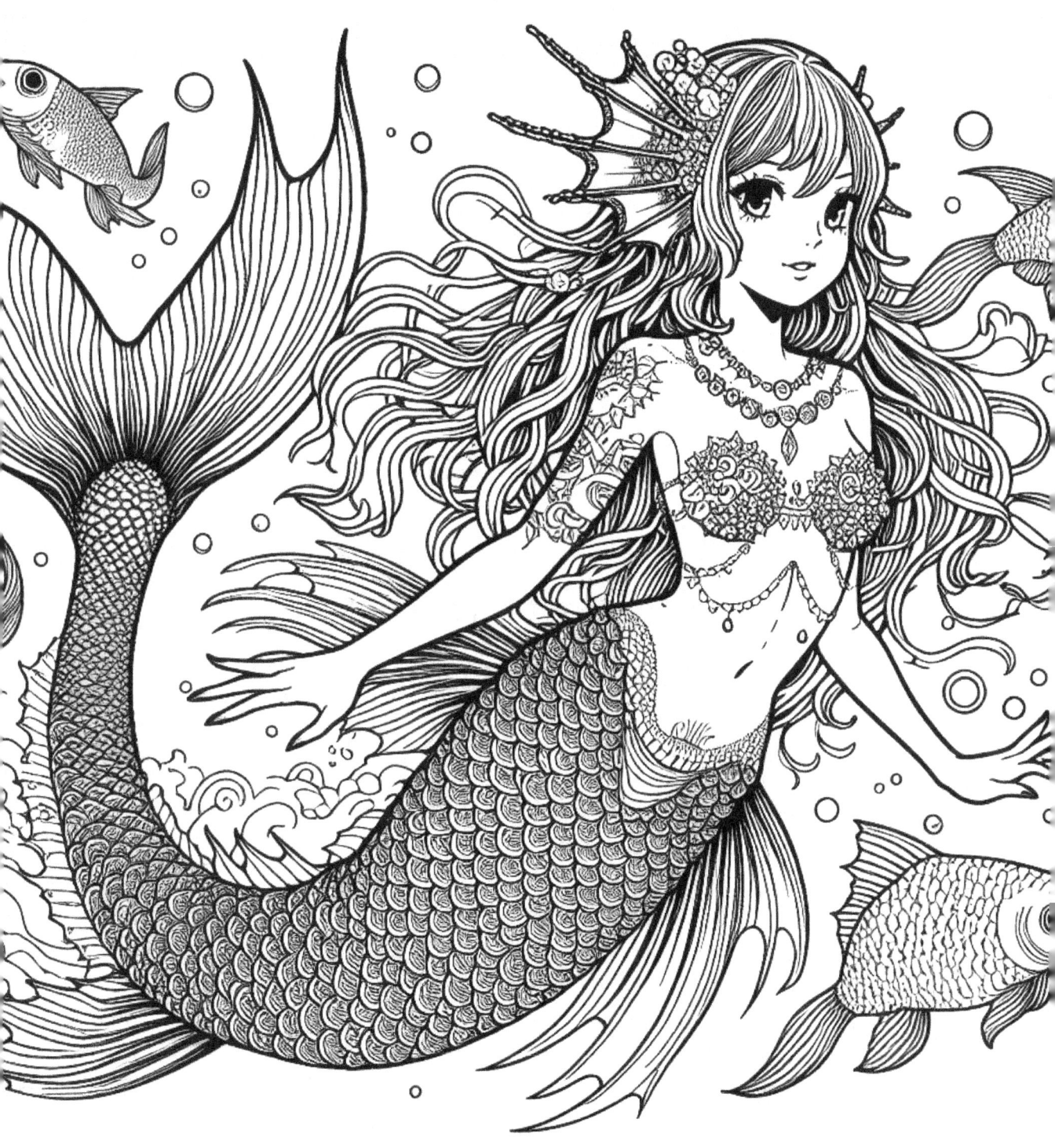

Japan

Ningyo

They were water monsters with
human upper bodies and fish tails,
who could foresee the future, but
also ate humans

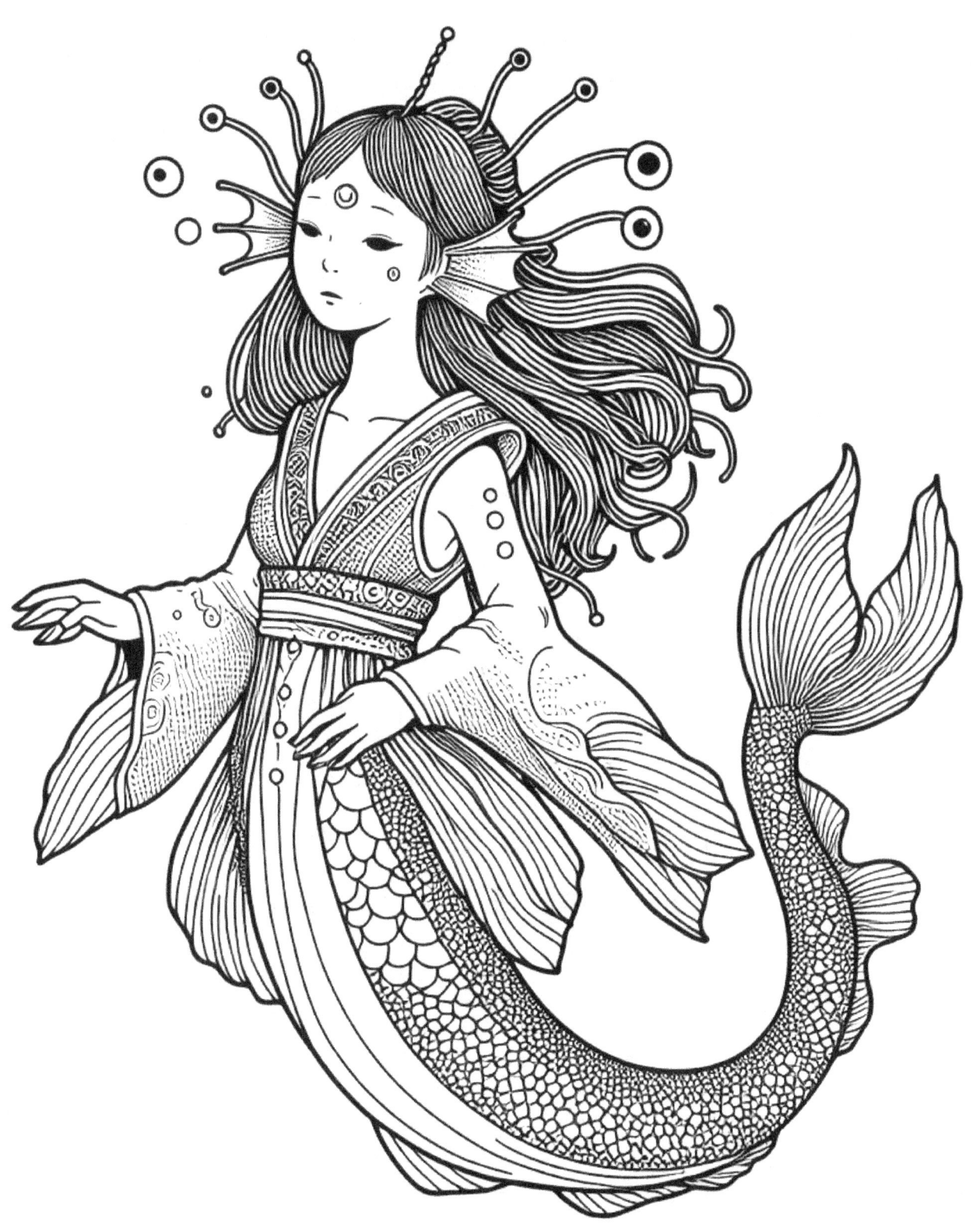

Japan

Ning Ning

They were water monsters with
human upper bodies and fish tails,
who could transform into humans,
and fell in love with humans, but
would disappear if their true identity
was discovered

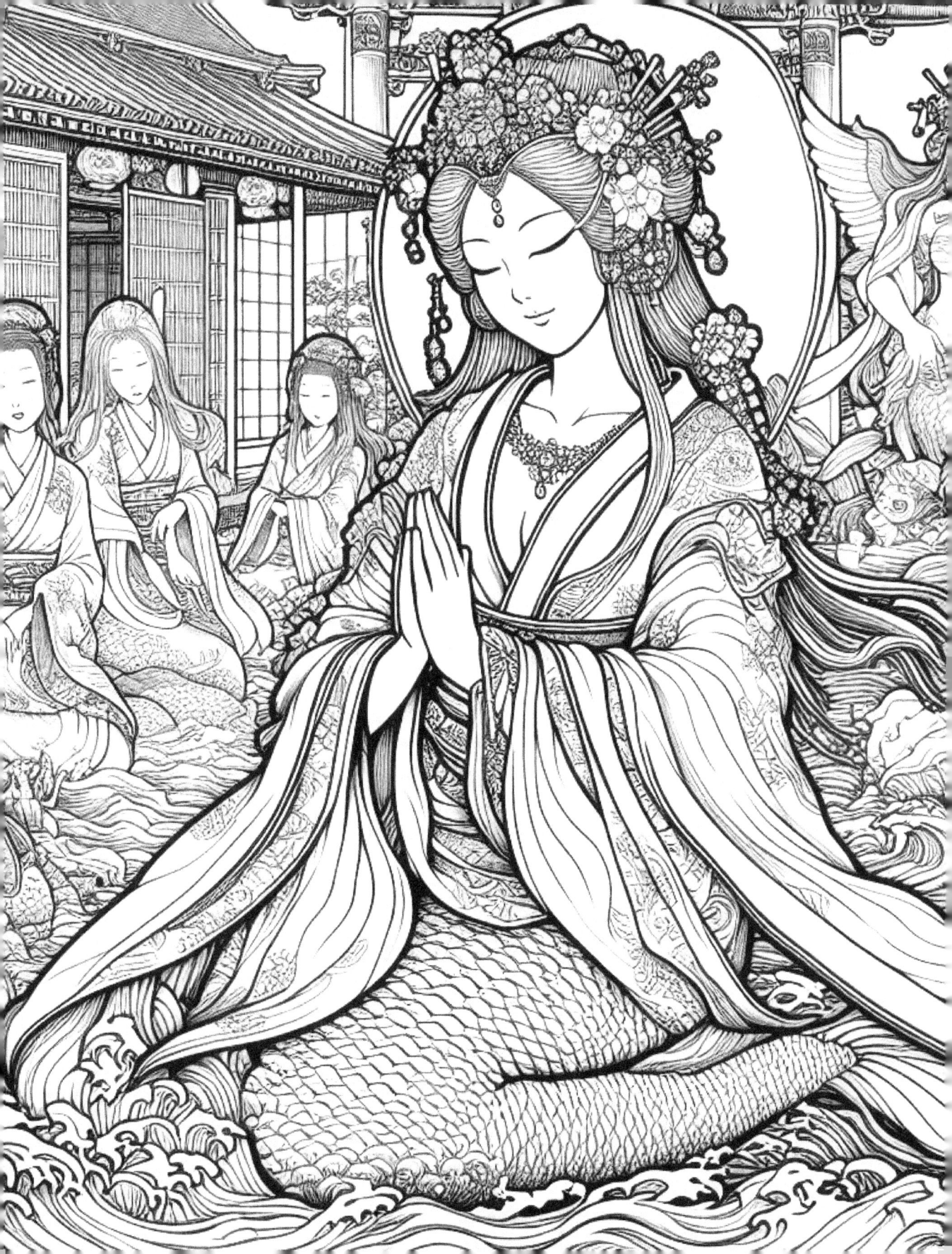

Japan

Yaobikuni

She was a long-lived woman who lived for eight hundred years, and remained young and beautiful, because she ate mermaid flesh, and was considered the founder of Wakasa province

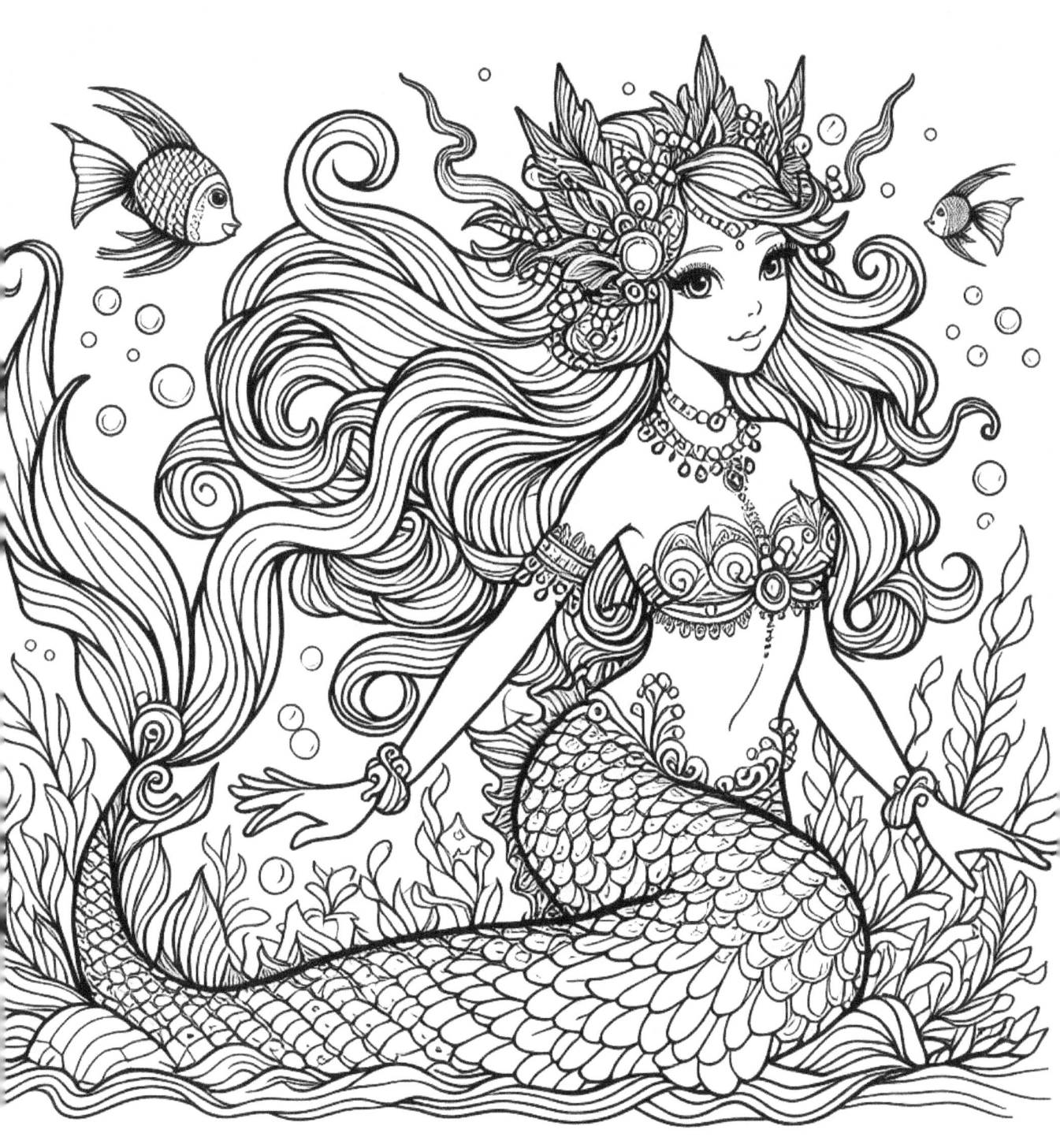

India

Amizuma

Amizuma is a mystical creature that
is half human, half fish, and is said
to be the wife or daughter of the sea
god Varuna, with a beautiful face
and a fish's tail. Sea wives like to
play in the sea and sometimes go
ashore to socialize with humans.
Some sea wives will fall in love with
humans and even give up their lives
in the ocean for the sake of humans

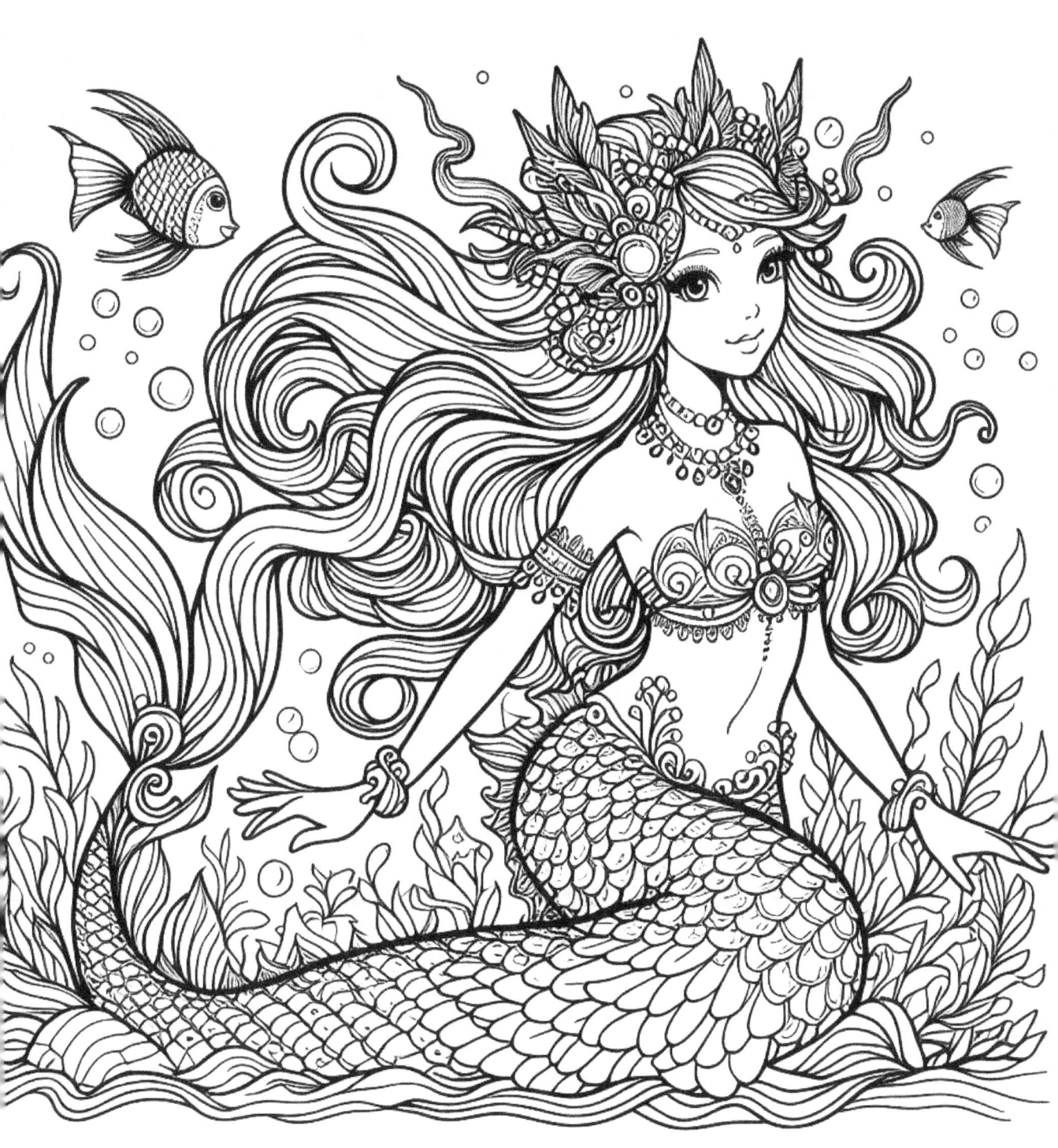

India

Amizuma

Amizuma is a mystical creature that is half human, half fish, and is said to be the wife or daughter of the sea god Varuna, with a beautiful face and a fish's tail. Sea wives like to play in the sea and sometimes go ashore to socialize with humans. Some sea wives will fall in love with humans and even give up their lives in the ocean for the sake of humans